Volume 2

"Near The Knuckle Chuckle"

**Also available from our
2003 collection:**

Lorenzo Amoruso: LA Confidential

The 2003 Crossword Book

Tam Cowan's JOKE BOOK

Volume 2

 "Near The Knuckle Chuckle"

First published 2002
by the Scottish Daily Record and Sunday Mail Ltd

ISBN 0-9544202-0-9

British Library Cataloguing in Publishing Data:
A catalogue record for this book is available
from the British Library.

Printed and bound in Great Britain

AS a youngster Tam Cowan was a regular in his school football team and a regional verse-speaking champion. But it was when he reached his late teens that Tam discovered his true talents – writing jokes and eating curries. After contributing material to Little and Large, Roy Hudd and Naked Video, Tam began writing about his favourite sport – football. His success in print led to him presenting the football show Off The Ball on Radio Scotland. Today Tam's popular football column appears twice a week in the Daily Record. He has also transferred his unique brand of football humour to the small screen with his Offside programme on BBC1 Scotland. Tam's previous TV outings include Taxi For Cowan – a comedy travelogue around Scotland.

In tandem to his media career, Tam has tirelessly kept eating and contributes a weekly restaurant review column to the Daily Record's Saturday Magazine.

When not working, Tam relaxes by watching Motherwell FC, listening to Englebert Humperdink, and making roasted cheese on the grill. Tam's favourite holiday destinations are Las Vegas and Rothesay.

1

Animal Crackers

Jokes from the animal kingdom

A little rabbit is happily running through the forest when he stumbles upon a giraffe rolling a joint. The rabbit looks at her and says, "Giraffe my friend, why do you do this? Come with me running through the forest, you'll feel so much better!"

The giraffe looks at him, looks at the joint, tosses it and goes off running with the rabbit.

Then they come across an elephant doing drugs, so the rabbit again says, "Elephant my friend, why do you do this? Think about your health! Come running with us through the pretty forest, you'll feel so good!"

The elephant looks at them, looks at his razor, mirror and all, then tosses them and starts running with the rabbit and giraffe.

The three animals then come across a lion about to do some heroin. "Lion my friend, why do you do this? Think about your health! Come running with us through the sunny forest, you will feel so good!"

The lion looks at him, puts down his needle, and starts to beat the crap out of the little rabbit.

The giraffe and elephant watch in horror, and ask him "Lion, why did you do this? He was merely trying to help us all!"

The lion answers, "Every time he's on Ecstasy that little bugger makes me run around the forest like an idiot for hours!"

A man walks into a country pub and orders a drink.

A few minutes later, a large shire horse comes trotting in, sits at a table, crosses its legs and orders a cup of coffee.

The man was gobsmacked, and asks the barman if he thought it was a little strange.

"Very strange," the barman replies. "Usually he has a pint."

An ant and an elephant have just spent a night of passion with each other when suddenly, the elephant drops down dead.

"Just my luck," says the ant, "One night of passion and I spend a lifetime digging a grave."

A three legged dog walks into a saloon in the Wild West. He staggers up to the bar, orders a Sasparilla and says,"OK, folks, I'm looking for the man who shot my paw."

A man walks into a pub with a pig under his arm. The barman says, "That's the ugliest looking animal I've ever seen. Where did you find it?"

"I won it in a raffle," says the pig.

A zoo managed to get one of an endangered species of gorilla. The beast is bad tempered and very difficult to handle. Upon further investigation, the zoo keepers find out that the female gorilla is in heat.

This of course is a bit of a problem since none of her species are at the zoo.

Then, one of the zoo keepers remember that one of the zoo workers, an Irishman called Finbar, has a bit of a reputation of being a ladies man who has left hundreds of women satisfied.

They ask him if he'll screw the gorilla for £500?

Finbar asks the zoo keepers for a night to think about the proposition. The following day he says he'll do it, but with three conditions.

"Firstly, I don't want to kiss her. Secondly, I want any offspring to be raised Roman Catholic."

The zoo keepers agrees to the first two conditions but is curious to hear the third condition.

"Well," says Finbar, "you're going to have to give me time to raise the £500."

Where do you find a cat with no legs?
Exactly where you left it.

Why do seagulls fly over the sea?
If they flew over the bay they'd be bagels.

Why do birds fly South for the Winter?
Because it's too far to walk.

One day a tiger is moping about the jungle a wee bit bored. Suddenly he spots a monkey up a tree so he says: "Hey there monkey, do you wanna come down here and have a chat, I'm really bored?"

"Do you think I'm stupid?" asked the monkey, "I know if I come down there, you'll eat me."

"No, no, no!" said the tiger, "Honestly, I only want to talk."

"OK," says the monkey, "tell ya what, if you tie yourself up, I'll come down, ok?"

The tiger proceeds to tie himself up and calls the monkey down.

The monkey looks a nervous wreck so the tiger says, "Hey, there's no need to be scared, look, I'm all tied up I couldn't hurt you even if I wanted to."

"That's not why I'm nervous." said the monkey.

"I've never shagged a tiger before."

**What has four legs and an arm?
A happy pit-bull!!!**

Davie was a garage petrol attendant. One day he was filling up another car, when he spotted three penguins sitting on the backseat of the car. Davie asked the driver: "What's up with those penguins?"

The man in the car replied: "I found them by the side of the road. But to tell you the truth, I have no idea what to do with them."

Davie wasn't the sharpest tool in the box, but after a few minutes of hard thinking he came up with a pretty good idea: "You should take them to the zoo," he said.

"Great idea," the man in the car smiled and drove away.

The next day the man with the car was back at Davie's petrol station. And the penguins were still in the back seat of the car!

"Hey, they're still here! I thought you were going to take them to the zoo," Davie said.

"Oh, I did," said the driver, "and we had a great time! Today I'm taking them to the beach."

Why do hens lay eggs?
Because if they dropped them, they would break.

What did the Cinderella fish wear to the ball?
Glass flippers.

How do you make a cat go WOOF?
Douse it in petrol and throw a match at it!

A vicar wanted to buy a parrot and asks the shopkeeper if he was sure the parrot didn't swear.

"No," replied the shopkeeper, "It's a religious parrot. It would never ever swear. He can even recite the Lords prayer when you pull his right leg."

The vicar asks, "What happens if you pull the left leg?"

"Well," replies the shopkeeper, "He sings one of his favourite Hymns."

"And what if I pull both legs?" asks the vicar.

"I fall of my f***ing perch you asshole!" screeches the parrot.

A farmer is a bit pissed off at the small number of eggs that his hens had been laying, so he decides to buy a new cockerel to liven the hen-house up a bit.

He goes to market the next day and spots a fine looking cockerel.

"How much for that fine specimen?" asks the farmer.

"Oh no, no" replies the cockerels owner, "That bird is obsessed with sex. I've never seen anything like it!"

The farmer thinks that this cockerel sounds perfect and persuades the guy to sell it to him.

As soon as the farmer gets the cockerel on the farm, it jumps into the hen-house and mounts all of the hens five times over. Then, it jumps into the duck pond and gives all of the ducks a proper seeing to. Next, the sex-crazed beast leaps over the fence and proceeds to shag all the geese.

This continued for five days solid. That afternoon, the farmer finds the cockerel lying on its back in the middle of the yard and there are vultures flying overhead ready to feast on the knackered beast.

"Well, well, well, serves you right you dirty little bugger." says the farmer, at which point the cockerel points up to the sky and says: "Shhhh."

What's grey on the inside and red on the outside?
An elephant turned inside out.

Two guys are standing on the white cliffs of Dover with their arms outstretched. One guy has a row of budgies lined up on his arms and the other has a row of parrots. After a while they both leap from the cliff and sure enough plunge to the rocky shore below.

Later that day in hospital, one guy says,"Well, I didn't think that budgie-jumping was all it's cracked up to be."

The other guy says, "You're right. And I'm not to keen on this parrot gliding either."

A farmer was sitting in his yard eating a Cornish pastie, when a hen whizzed past, quickly followed by a cockerel. Suddenly, the cockerel screeched to a halt and began pecking at the farmer's Cornish pastie.

"Jeez," said the farmer, "I hope I never get that hungry!"

What side of a chicken has the most feathers?
The outside

A guy was astonished when he found his friend playing chess with his dog.

"I can't believe my eyes!" he said. "That has got to be the smartest dog I have ever seen."

His friend shook his head, "Nah, he's not that smart. I've beaten him three times out of five."

An elephant was down by the watering hole in the Savannah when he saw a turtle out of the corner of his eye. The elephant leapt into the air and landed right on top of the turtle, squishing it completely.

A monkey who had seen the horrific incident said, "Oh man, that was a terrible thing to do. Why on earth did you squish that poor turtle?"

The elephant said, "That bugger gave me a nasty bite on the leg 60 years ago. I was getting my revenge."

"Wow!" explained the monkey, "You must have a fantastic memory!"

The elephant nodded and said, "Yup, I have turtle recall!"

Two rats were sitting behind a restaurant eating their way through the bins when one said to the other, "Have you seen that new restaurant down the bottom of the road? It's so clean. The floors are spotless, the kitchens are gleaming. It's so hygienic." "Please," says the other rat, "Not while I'm eating!"

A door to door salesman turned up at a house determined to make a sale. He rang the doorbell and a young boy answered.

"Hi there, is your mummy or daddy in?".

"The boy just stood there staring without saying a word.

"Where are they then?" asked the slightly confused salesman.

The little boy pointed up the stairs to the bedroom.

The salesman adjusted his tie and opened the bedroom door.

What he saw next horrified him.

A woman was lying in the bed naked with a donkey by her side.

"AAAARRRRGGGGGHHHH" screamed the salesman as he ran down the stairs.

As he got to the door he said to the little boy, "Do you know what's going on up there? Doesn't it bother you?"

The little boy looked at him and said, "N-a-a-a-a."

There had been a terrible bus accident one day outside Edinburgh Zoo. No-one survived except a little monkey.

When the police arrived at the scene they tried to interview the monkey with hand gestures. The monkey managed to understand some of the questions.

The police officer asked the monkey what the people on the bus had been doing before it crashed.

The monkey started to dance around: Meaning that the people on the bus had been having fun.

The officer then asked what else they had been doing. The monkey responded by moving his hand to his mouth as if he was holding a bottle: meaning the people had been drinking.

"Anything else?" asked the officer.

The monkey nodded and started making pelvic thrusts indicating the people had been having sex.

"Jesus wept!" exclaimed the officer. "Who the hell was driving the bus?"

The monkey cheerfully started to move his arms as if turning a wheel...

Why do Aberdonians wear kilts?
So the sheep won't hear the zip.

What do you get if you cross an onion with a donkey?

A piece of ass that will bring tears to your eyes.

How do you spot a gay termite?
He only eats woodpeckers.

What is meaner than a pit-bull with a sexually transmitted disease?
Whatever gave it the sexually transmitted disease in the first place.

How do monkeys pick up the latest gossip?
Through the apevine.

Two Aberdonians were flying their new flock of sheep to their farm when the engines of the plane cut out sending the plane into a downwards spiral.
"Quick, grab a parachute and jump!" screamed one of the men.
"What about the sheep?" asked the other.
"F*** the sheep!" screams the other.
"Do you think we have time?" responds the other.

So this baby seal walks into a club. Bloody tragic!

A seal walks into a bar.
"What can I get ya little fella?" asks the barman.
"Anything except a Canadian Club," replies the seal.

One morning Daddy Bear came down to breakfast to find his porridge bowl empty.

"Somebody's been eating my porridge!" he said.

"Someone's been eating my porridge too!" said Baby Bear.

Just then, Mummy Bear came out of the kitchen and said, "You stupid idiots. I haven't made it yet!"

A young man finds a job in a circus. He's willing to do almost anything to earn a couple of quid.

The circus owner decided that he might make a good lion tamer. The guy says he'll give it a go although he's never done anything like it before.

The owner takes him to the practice cage to watch how the professionals do it.

When they get there, the lion tamer and his beautiful assistant are just starting their rehearsal.

The beautiful assistant removes her cloak to reveal a gorgeous body.

The lion purred with delight, crept towards her and started to lick her face.

"Well", said the owner to the young man, "do you think you could do that?"

"I'm sure I could", said the young man, "but you'll have to get that lion out of there first!"

Paddy and Mick were shopping for horses. When they each found a horse they liked, they found they had a bit of a problem.

"How will we tell the horses apart?" asked Paddy.

"I know" said Mick, "We'll clip one of the horses ears."

"No," said Paddy, "that would hurt the horse."

"OK" said Mick, "I'll cut off my horses tail."

"No, no" said Paddy, "The horse needs it's tail to brush flies away."

"OK," said Mick, "I think we should brand them. I'll put a huge X on my horse's backside!"

"No," said Paddy, "A horse is a beautiful creature, that wouldn't be nice."

"I've got it," said Mick. "You take the black one and I'll take the white one!"

A snake goes to a bar for a couple of halfs but the landlord shouts, "Get the hell outa here! I'm not serving you."

"Why not?," asks the snake.

"Because you can't hold your drink," replies the landlord.

A fish staggers into a bar.
"What can I get you?" asks the barman.
The fish croaks, "Water!"

A young guy joins the Foreign Legion and is sent to live in the Sahara Desert.

After a few months with no female contact, he visits his commander and says, "I haven't had sex for months. Can you point me in the right direction?"

"Well", says the commander, "You can borrow my camel anytime you like."

The young man declines the offer.

Six months later, he is really frustrated, so he visits the commander again.

"Right, I'm bloody desperate" says young man, "Is the offer still on about the camel?"

"Of course it is" says the commander, "She's round at the back of the compound."

The young man runs round, grabs the camel and fires in.

The next day, the man thanks the commander who says, "Any time. It's much quicker to the local brothel by camel, isn't it?"

What do you get if you cross a prostitute with an elephant?

A whore that will shag you for peanuts and won't forget you afterwards.

A blind man was waiting to cross the road when his guide dog pissed on his leg. He reached into his pocket, took out a biscuit and gave it to the dog.

A woman who'd seen the incident said, "You're a very tolerant man. Not many people would have reacted with such kindness."

"I'm not that tolerant" replied the blind man. "I'm just finding out where his mouth is so I can kick him in the balls."

Two tall trees are standing in the woods when a young tree begins to grow between them.

One tree says to the other, "Is that a son of a Beech or a son of a Birch?"

The other tree shakes its branches and says that he doesn't know.

A while later a Woodpecker lands on the small tree. One of the tall trees says, "Hey you, Mr Woodpecker, you know your trees. Tell me, is that small tree a son of a Beech or a son of a Birch?

The Woodpecker takes a nibble of the small tree and says, "It's neither. That tree is the best piece of Ash I've ever had my pecker in."

What is bright orange and sounds like a parrot? A carrot.

At a conference on the supernatural, one of the speakers asked, "How many people here have seen a ghost?" Every one of the crowd put up their hands.

"Now tell me, how many of you have had some sort of interaction with a ghost?" Half of the gathered crowd raised their hands.

"How many of you have had some sort of physical contact with a ghost?" He asked.

Five people in the room put their hands in the air.

"That's very interesting," said the speaker.

"Let's take it a stage further then. How many people here have had sex with a ghost?"

One hand shot up in the air, much to the amazement of the crowd. Everyone in the hall turned and stared at the man with wonder in their eyes.

"Excuse me sir," said the speaker, "You are actually telling us you have slept with a ghost?"

The guy went bright red and lowered his hand slowly and said, "Oh, I'm sorry. I thought you said goat."

How can you tell if you're in an elevator with an elephant?
You can smell the peanuts on its breath.

An Aberdonian, a sheep and a dog were survivors of a terrible shipwreck. They found themselves stranded on a desert island. After being there for a while, they got into the habit of going to the beach every evening to watch the sun go down.

One particular evening the sky was red with beautiful cirrus clouds, the breeze was warm and gentle; a perfect night for romance. As they sat there, the sheep started looking better and better to the Aberdonian. Soon, he leaned over to the sheep and put his arm around it. But the dog got jealous, growling fiercely until the Aberdonian took his arm from around the sheep.

After that, the three of them continued to enjoy the sunsets together but there was no more cuddling.

A few weeks passed, and lo and behold, there was another shipwreck. The only survivor was a beautiful young woman, the most beautiful woman the Aberdonian had ever seen.

She was in a pretty bad way when they rescued her, and they slowly nursed her back to health. When the young maiden was well enough, they introduced her to the evening ritual.

It was another beautiful evening, red sky, cirrus clouds, a warm and gentle breeze; perfect for a night of romance. Pretty soon, the Aberdonian started to get "those feelings" again.

He fought them as long as he could, but he finally gave in and leaned over to the young woman, and whispered in her ear....

"Would you mind taking the dog for a walk?"

A ventriloquist was on holiday up in Aberdeenshire where he met a local farmer. The ventriloquist decided to have a wee bit of fun at the farmers expense.

"Excuse me sir," said the ventriloquist, "can I have a word with your dog please?"

"The dog doesn't talk you idiot," replied the farmer.

"You may be surprised," says the ventriloquist.

"Hi there Mr Dog, how does the farmer treat you?"

"Hi there," says the dog, "He treats me really well. He gives me plenty to eat and every Friday he lets me run around the fields at my leisure and I get a nice bit of steak too on a Saturday."

The farmer is amazed, he can hardly believe what he's hearing.

"Can I talk to your horse please?" asks the ventriloquist.

"The horse can't talk." replies the farmer.

"Hey, horse, how does the farmer treat you?" asks the ventriloquist.

"He's pretty good to me," replies the horse. "He gives me plenty of space to gallop around in and he keeps me sheltered at night in a nice warm stable with plenty to eat and drink."

"How about I have a word with your sheep," says the ventriloquist.

"Erm, cough, cough" splutters the farmer, "Sheep lie."

Have you heard about the wallet that's made of an elephant foreskin?
   When you rub it, it turns into a briefcase!

What did the vet say to the dog who kept licking his balls?
   Thanks very much, darling.

Why do hummingbirds hum?
   Because they don't know the words.

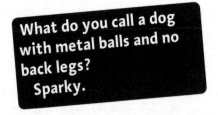

What do you call a dog with metal balls and no back legs?
   Sparky.

How can you tell if an elephant has been in your fridge?
   There are footprints in the butter.

How do you know if there have been two elephants in you fridge?
There are two sets of footprints in your butter.

How do you know if there have been three elephants in your fridge?
You can't get the door closed.

Why did the turtle cross the road?
To get to the Shell garage.

Why do gorillas wear pink tennis shoes?
Because the white ones get dirty to quickly.

Three rats are sitting in a bar having a few pints and chatting away when one of them says, "I'm so hard that I once ate a whole bag of rat poison."
  The second rat says, "That's nothing. I'm so hard, I once was caught in a trap. I managed to gnaw my way through my leg, free myself and then escape."
  The third rat slides off his bar stool and says, "Right lads, I'm away home to shag the cat!"

Why do elephants paint their toenails red?
So no-one will see them when they hide in cherry trees.

Why don't animals play Poker in the Savannah?
There are too many cheetahs.

Why didn't the jungle animals invite the giraffes to their Christmas party?
Because they were a pain in the neck to talk to.

An old woman managed to save the life of a fairy. To repay the favour, the fairy said she would grant the woman three wishes.

For her first wish, the old woman asked to become young and beautiful. POOF! The old woman became young and beautiful.

For the second wish, the old woman asked to become the richest person on earth. POOF! The old woman became the richest person on earth.

For her third and final wish, the old woman asked if her cat could be turned into the most handsome man on earth. POOF! The cat turned into the most handsome man on earth.

After the fairy left, the handsome man said to the beautiful, young woman, "I bet you're sorry you had me neutered three years ago!"

Why is Turtle Wax so expensive?
Because their ears are so small.

Why do elephants have Big Ears?
Because Noddy wouldn't pay the ransom.

A man visited his doctor about getting his penis enlarged. The procedure was a tricky one and involved grafting an elephant's trunk onto the man's chopper.

After the operation, he and his girlfriend visited a very expensive restaurant to celebrate the successful operation.

As they started their first course, the man's penis crept out of his trousers, grabbed a bread roll off the table and disappeared back under the table.

The girlfriend was a bit shocked to say the least, but tried to ignore the fact and continued with her meal.

Two minutes later, the penis reappeared and grabbed another bread roll before disappearing under the table.

The girlfriend said, "I don't believe what I just saw. Can you do it again?"

The man, who was looking a bit uncomfortable, said, "I'd like to, but I don't think I could cram another bread roll up my backside!"

How do you make an elephant float?
It takes eight elephants, ten tons of chocolate, five tons of ice cream, three tons of bananas...

**What do you call a cow that's had an abortion?
Decalfinated.**

A herd of cattle was standing on a hill when there was an earthquake. All of the cows fell to the ground but the bull remained standing.

The farmer asked the bull, "How come you didn't fall down like the rest of the herd?"

The bull replied, "We bulls wobble, but we don't fall down."

**Why couldn't the pony speak?
Because he was a little hoarse.**

Do you know what mothballs smell like?
Yes!
Really. How did you get their little legs apart?

**What do you call 14 rabbits walking backward?
A receding hairline.**

What's the difference between a poodle humping
your leg and a pit-bull humping your leg?
The pit-bull gets to finish!

2

What's up Doc?

Jokes from the medical world

A couple age 67, went to the doctor's office. The doctor asked, "What can I do for you?" The man said, "Doctor, Will you watch us make love?" The doctor looked puzzled but agreed.

When the couple finished, the Doctor said "There's nothing wrong with the way you make love." And he charged them £10. This happened for several weeks in a row. The couple would make an appointment, make love, and then leave.

Finally the Doctor asked, "Just exactly what are you trying to find out?" The old man said, "We're not trying to find out anything. She is married and we can't go to her house. I'm married and we can't go to my house. The Holiday Inn charges £22, the Hilton charges £27 so we do it here for £10 and I get £8 back from the social for every visit to the doctor's.

A dentist informed his patient that she needed root canal treatment.

"Oh my God," replied the woman, "I'd rather have a baby."

"Well," said the dentist, "You had better make up your mind before I finish adjusting the chair."

After a few months in the Far East, a man arrives home to discover that he has contracted a strange, luminous disease in his nether regions.

He rushes to see his doctor and is given the bad news that his "Old Man" will have to be amputated.

Shocked and in distress, he visits all the top doctors in Europe but is given the same answer by all of them...amputation!

As a last resort, he goes to see an old witch doctor living in deepest Africa.

Upon seeing the mans' todger, the witch doctor says, "Don't worry, amputation will not be necessary."

The man is delighted, but asks,"Are you sure? I went all over Europe and every doctor I saw said amputation was the only solution."

"What do they know?" said the witch doctor, "Any doctor worth his salt would have told you that it will drop off itself in three to four weeks."

A man goes to the hospital to get a leg amputated. The doctor's can't remember what leg was due to be cut off, so they decide to chop off both legs.

The patient wakes up and is furious so he decides to sue the hospital.

The case was thrown out of court because the man didn't have a leg to stand on.

As the paramedic arrived on the accident site, he found that the entire drivers side of the Porche had been ripped away, taking with it the drivers arm. The injured driver was a lawyer and was obviously in shock. He kept screaming, "My car, my beautiful car." The paramedic tried to calm the lawyer down and said, "Excuse me sir, but I think you should be more concerned about your arm than your car."

The driver looked down to where his arm had been and screamed, "My Rolex! My Rolex!"

A woman went to the doctor for a follow up visit after he had prescribed testosterone for her. She was a little concerned about the side effects.

"Doctor, the hormone that you've given me has been a huge help but I'm afraid you might have given me too much. I've started growing hair in places I've never grown hair before."

The doctor said, "A little hair growth is a perfectly normal side effect of testosterone. Just exactly where has it appeared?"

"On my balls!"

A man had been suffering from a really bad cold for a couple of weeks and finally decided to go see his doctor. The doc gives the guy some tablets. A week later, the guy returns in a worse state. The doctor is baffled by the illness and makes a note of it in his medical journal as "Coldus Incurabilis"

"OK," says the doc, "what I want you to do tonight is to strip naked and sit in front of an open window."

"WHAT?" yelled the patient. "I'll catch pneumonia!"

"Pneumonia is fine," replies the doctor. "I can treat pneumonia."

Three patients in a mental institution are preparing for an examination by the head psychiatrist. If the patients pass the exam, they will be released and if they fail they will have to spend another 10 years in a padded cell.

The three patients are taken to a high diving board above an empty swimming pool.

The first patient jumps and breaks both of his legs and both of his arms.

The second guy jumps head first and breaks his neck.

The third patient peers down and backs away from the board.

"Congratulations, well done," says the head psychiatrist. "You're a free man, but tell me why you didn't jump?"

"Well," said the patient, "I can't swim."

A trendy new clinic opened up in the centre of Glasgow. Wanting to be a bit different and creative, it was decided that each doctor's office door would be representative of their practice.

The eye doctor had a peep-hole, the psychiatrist's door was painted with many different colours and the orthopaedist's door had a broken hinge. As for the gynaecologist's door, it was left open ... just a crack.

A doctor began his examination of a pensioner by asking him what brought him to the hospital. The old man looked a wee bit bemused and said, "Why, by ambulance of course!"

A woman gives birth to identical twins and unfortunately can't look after them, so she gave them up for adoption. One goes to a family in Egypt and is named Amhal. The other twin goes to Spain and is named Juan.

Years later she receives a photo of Juan, who has become a very successful businessman.

Desperate to see her other son, the mother phones her doctor to see if he knows where Amhal lives so she can get in touch with him.

"Look," said the doctor, "I'll be honest with you, I don't know where Amhal is now."

The mother is distraught.

"There, there," says the doctor, "Don't worry, they are twins, if you've seen Juan, you've seen Ahmal."

A guy visits his doctors and says, "Hey doc, I feel like I've turned into a cowboy."

"And how long have you been feeling like this?" asks the doctor.

"Oh, about a YEEEEEHHHAAAAAA" shouts the man.

An inmate went to see the prison doctor and was dismayed to be told he needed to have a kidney removed.

"Come on doc, this is getting ridiculous. You've already taken my tonsils, my spleen, my gall-bladder and part of my intestines! I only came to see you because I wanted you to get me out of here."

The doctor replied, "That's exactly what I am doing...bit by bit."

Have you heard the one about the nurse who swallowed a scalpel by mistake? She gave herself a tonsillectomy, an appendectomy and a hysterectomy and circumcised three of the doctors.

"Doctor, should I file my nails?" asked the woman.

"No, you should throw them away like everyone else." replied the doctor.

How can you tell the head nurse?
She's the one with scuffed knees.

A man visits his doctor because he can't get his wife pregnant. The doctor is a little taken aback because the man is 82 years old. The doctor asks the man to produce a sperm sample and gives him a jar.

Two days later, the man returns to the doctor's surgery and gives the doctor an empty jar.

"This is empty," said the doctor, "I asked you to provide a sample of your sperm."

"Well doc, first I tried it with my left hand but that didn't work. So then I tried it with my right hand but that didn't work either, so I asked my wife to help. She is a good deal younger than me so she tried with both her hands but still nothing was happening. Then she tried with her mouth but still nothing. Then, as a last resort we got our next door neighbour to come round and give it a whirl but still no joy even with the three of us at it."

"Nothing?" asked the doctor a little bit surprised.

"Listen doc, we tried and tried, but no matter what we did none of us could get the bloody lid of that jar!"

What do you call a man who ignores doctors?
The Health Secretary.

Did you hear about the doctor who had his medical license taken away because he was having sex with his patients?

Yeah, it's a shame because he was one of the best Vets in the country.

Patient: "Doc, if I give up wine, women and song will it make me live longer?"
Doctor: "No, it will just seem that way."

A little boy swallows a can opener and his mum rushes him to the hospital.

"Don't panic Mrs Munro, he'll be alright."

"Yes but how do I open the tin of beans while the toast is getting cold?" replies the mother.

A woman visits the dentist. As he begins working, she grabs his nuts really tightly."

"Excuse me miss, but you seem to have a firm grip on my rab haws."

"That right, so we'll be very careful not to hurt each other!"

An old man visits his local hospital to get a new form of plastic surgery done where they stretch your skin up to get rid of all the wrinkles.

On his way out of the hospital after the operation he meets one of his old friends who doesn't recognise him.

"Wow Jimmy, you look 30 years younger. I didn't realise you had a dimple on your chin."

"That's not a dimple, that's my bellybutton." replied Jimmy. "And if you think that's funny, you should see what I'm using for a tie!"

Patient: "Doctor, I keep thinking I'm a pack of cards."
Doctor: "Sit over there. I'll deal with you later."

Patient: "Will the operation hurt in this new private hospital?"
Doctor: "Only when you receive the final bill."

"Ooooh Doctor," moaned the woman to the psychitrist. "Everyone thinks I'm a dirty nympho."
"I understand fully," replied the psychitrist, "but I'll be able to make a better assessment if you let go of my cock."

A patient visits a psychiatrist. The psychiatrist gives him a test which involves looking at different coloured cards and the patient has to tell the psychiatrist what he sees.

The first card shows a rectangle with a dot in the middle.

"It looks like two people having sex in a rectangular room," the patient replies.

The second card shows a circle with a dot in the middle.

"That looks like two people having sex in a circular room," the patient replies.

The third card shows a triangle with a dot in the middle.

The patient says: "What the hell are you up to? Are you some sort of pervert?"

Patient: "Doctor, is it serious?"
Doctor: "Well, lets just say you shouldn't start any big books."

Patient: "Doctor, I keep thinking I'm a white snooker ball."
Doctor: "Get to the end of the queue."

What is the proper term for the circumcision of a rabbit?
A hare cut.

An Irishman goes to see his doctor because when he pokes himself on the head, arm, shoulder and chest he gets a terrible shooting pain.
After a careful examination, the doctor tells him that his index finger is broken.

Did you hear about the two blood cells called Romeo and Juliet?
Their love was in vein.

3

Battle of the sexes

Jokes about men and women

A new bride was a bit embarrassed about being identified as a honeymooner. So when she and her new husband pulled up at the hotel, she asked him if they could make it appear as though they had been married for years.

"Sure," he said, "you can carry the cases."

How many men does it take to wallpaper a living room?

Only four, but you have to slice them really thinly.

> **Marriage teaches you loyalty, patience, perserverence, understanding and many other things you would't need if you had stayed single.**

Two guys were talking in a bar one evening.

"How was your Honeymoon?" Steve asked.

"Great," said Jimmy. "Until I woke up on the first morning. I forgot where I was and said to my wife. "You were wonderful. Here's £100."

"Well," said Steve "She might not know you thought she was a prostitute."

"I know," said Jimmy, "but my wife gave me £50 back and said, "Here's your change.""

A man returns home early from work to find his wife making passionate love to a complete stranger in their bedroom.

Outraged, the man asks, "What the Hell do you think you're doing?"

"See" says his wife to her lover,"I told you he was thick."

A priest and a nun were returning from a church convention when their car broke down in the middle of nowhere.

They managed to find a cheap guesthouse but there was only one room available.

"Well," said the priest, "I don't think the good Lord would mind if we spent a night together under the circumstances. You take the bed and I'll sleep on the couch."

Late into the night, the nun said, "Excuse me father, but I'm terribly cold."

"Don't worry sister, I'll get you a blanket from the cupboard."

Ten minutes later the nun said, "Father, I'm still cold."

"OK, I'll get you another blanket from the cupboard." said the priest.

Ten minutes later, the nun said, "Father, I'm still really cold. I'm sure the Lord wouldn't mind if we acted like man and wife for one night."

"Your right," said the priest. "Get up and get your own bloody blankets!"

One rainy afternoon, a woman is in bed with her boyfriend while her husband is at work. Suddenly she hears his car in the driveway. She screams at the boyfriend, "Quick! Grab your clothes and jump out of the window!"

The boyfriend grabs his clothes and leaps out of the window and into the pouring rain.

When he lands, he finds himself in the middle of a charity half-marathon. He starts jogging along beside the other runners, naked and holding his clothes under one arm.

One of the runners asks him, "Do you always run in the nude?"

"I sure do," said the man, "I love the feeling of rain on my naked body."

Another runner then asks him, "Do you always carry your clothes with you when you go running?"

"Yup," replies the man. "When I've finished my run, I can get dressed straight away and head off home."

A third runner then asks him, "Do you always wear a condom when your running?"

The guy replies, "Only when it's raining"

A couple from Fife were in a hotel on their Honeymoon. They were ready to get down and dirty, when the new wife said to her husband, "I've never done this before, so please be gentle."

The husband sprang out of bed and hurried to the phone where he called his father for some advice.

"Dad, she's a Virgin, what the hell will I do?"

"Come on home, son. Leave her. If she's not good enough for her own family, then she's not good enough for ours."

Mickey Mouse was trying to convince the judge to grant him a divorce from Minnie. "I'm sorry Mickey," said the judge, "but claiming that Minnie is crazy is not a valid reason for me to grant a divorce."

"I didn't say she was crazy," said Mickey, "I said she was f***ing Goofy."

Two Irishmen were working on a building site. The foreman wouldn't give them a break and was always on at them to keep working.

One day, one of the Irishmen noticed that the foreman left every day at 3 o'clock every afternoon. So they started to leave at 3.15.

One day one of the men left at 3.15, arrived home and found his wife in bed with the foreman.

The next day he told his mate,"Listen, we can't knock off work early any more. Yesterday I almost got caught!"

A father was with his young son in the local park when they saw two dogs having sex. The boy asked his dad what they were doing.

The father said, "They're making a puppy, son."

A couple of days later, the boy walked in on his mum and dad who were having sex in the bedroom.

He asked his father what they were doing.

The father replied, "We're making a baby."

The young boy looked horrified and said, "Can you turn mummy over, I would much rather have a puppy."

What do you say to a blonde
with no arms and legs?
"Nice tits, darling."

Superman is flying across the skies of Manhattan when he sees his old flame Wonder Woman lying naked on the roof of her apartment building.

"Well, well, well," says Superman to himself, "I think I'll just nip down there and give her one for old times sake."

He flies down, shags her in super quick time and flies of again.

Wonder Woman says, "Christ what happened there?"

"I really don't know, but my arse is on fire!" replies the Invisible Man.

One morning, a guy walks up behind his missus and grabs her bottom. "You know something love, if you firmed this baby up, we could get rid of your industrial sized pants."

His wife is quite insulted by this but decides to say nothing.

The next morning the guy grabs hold of her left breast and says, "You know love, if you firmed these up we could get rid of your industrial sized bras."

The wife, unable to take any more abuse, grabs her husband's crotch and says, "Listen, If you firmed this up, we could get rid of the milkman, the postman and your brother!"

Which disease paralyses women from the waist down? Marriage.

Little Jimmy's dad picks him up one day after school. Jimmy has been tying out for a part in the latest school play and is very excited about it.

"Hey dad, I got a part in the play! I play a man who has been married to the same woman for over 30 years!"

"That's great son, I'm really proud of you. If you keep at it and try to become better, then one day I'm sure you'll get a speaking part."

Eleven people were hanging on a rope under a helicopter, ten men and one woman. The rope was not strong enough to carry them all, so they decided that one had to leave, because otherwise they were all going to fall.

They were unable to name the person until the woman held a very touching speech. She said that she would voluntarily let go off the rope, because as a woman she is used to giving up everything for her husband and kids, or for men in general, without ever getting anything in return.

As soon as she finished her speech, all men started clapping their hands.

A woman's husband had been slipping in and out of a coma for several months, yet she had stayed by his bedside every single day. One day, when he came to, he motioned for her to come nearer.

He whispered, eyes full of tears, "You know what? You've been with me all through the bad times. When I got fired, you were there to support me. When my business hit the rocks, you were there. When I lost the house, you were right there. When I got shot, you were by my side. When my health started failing, you were still by my side. And do you know what?"

"What dear?" She gently asked.

"You're bloody bad luck."

George and Margaret met each other for the first time and they were soon chatting like old friends. Later that night, George invited Margaret back to Motherwell for a bit of 'hide the sausage.'

Before long, there were making passionate love. As he was grinding away, George noticed that Margaret's toes curled up every time he thrust really hard.

After the deed had been done, George said, "Excuse me Margaret, but I couldn't help noticing when I thrust really hard your toes curled up. I must be a bit good in bed."

"Mmmmmm, the last time that happened, someone forgot to remove my tights." replied Margaret.

"My husband is like an angel," a woman said to her friend.
"You're lucky," replied the friend.
"Mine is still alive."

A bloke was in the boozer chatting to his mates.

"I had to phone Carstairs last night to check if any of the inmates had escaped recently."

One of his mates said, "Really, why was that then? Feeling a wee bit nervous?"

"Oh no, no," said the man, "Someone ran off with my wife last night and I just thought I'd check."

What is the definition of the perfect woman?
   A gorgeous, deaf and dumb, blonde nympho whose dad owns a boozer.

What is the difference between a woman and a volcano?
   A volcano doesn't fake eruptions.

Why are blondes like cornflakes?
   Because they're simple, easy and they taste good.

What do you call a woman who can suck an orange through a hose pipe?
   Darling!

A husband asked his wife if the Postman had come yet. She replied, "No, not yet but he has been puffing and panting quite a bit!"

Which disease paralyses women from the waist down?
   Marriage.

The doctor looked at the worried wife and said, "I'm afraid your husband is at death's door." The wife said, "Isn't there any way you could open it and shove the b**** through?"**

My ex-wife is an excellent laxative. If the sight of her doesn't make you crap yourself, she'll irritate the shit out of you in a couple of hours.

What is a bloke's idea of a fantastic 7-course meal?
A pizza and a six pack.

What do a clitoris, an anniversary and a toilet have in common?
  Men always miss them.

Why did God create man?
  Because a vibrator doesn't mow the lawn.

What do you call a woman without an asshole?
  Divorced.

How many men does it take to change a lightbulb?

Four. One to screw it in and three friends to brag about how they would have screwed it.

What is the most stupid part of a man's body?

The penis. It has a head without a brain, it hangs around with a bampot and it lives just round the corner from an arsehole.

A man comes home from an exhausting day at the office, plops down on the couch in front of the TV, and tells his wife, "Get me a beer before it starts." The wife sighs and gets him a beer. Fifteen minutes later, the man says, "Get me another beer before it starts." She looks cross, but fetches another beer and slams it down next to him. He finishes that beer and a few minutes later says, "Quick, get me another beer, it's going to start any minute."

The wife is furious. She yells at him, "Is that all you're going to do tonight? Drink beer and sit in front of that TV? You're nothing but a lazy, drunken, fat slob, and furthermore..." The man sighs and says: "It's started".

A young man and his wife go to the hospital to give birth to their new child. On arrival, the midwife prepares the room and ensures that the two are comfortable with the situation. The young man says that this is the greatest moment of his life and he wants to play a part in his new child's life.

His wife gives birth shortly after and the young man is overjoyed to have a beautiful baby boy. His wife is tired and the midwife takes the baby from her and says she will bathe him. The young man pipes up and says,

"No, I want to play a part in his life as of now, let me bathe him."

"Well, alright," replies the midwife, "come with me and I will show you where all the equipment is."

As the new father is preparing the bath the midwife says that she will pop out, get a cup of tea and return in two minutes. Baby and father are happy to be left alone.

On return however, the midwife sees the father with his index and middle finger in the baby's nose, forming neat figures of eight in the bath.

"What on earth are you doing!" screamed the shocked midwife, to which the father replied,

"I'm not putting my hand in that water, you ought to feel how bloody hot it is!"

A girl arrives home from university for Christmas. She yells: "Mum, mum, I've got a case of VD from university!"

"OK dear, put it in the cellar," says her mother. "your dad will drink anything."

A woman walks into a hardware store and asks the shopkeeper for a door hinge. The shopkeeper asks, "Do you need a screw for the hinge?"

The woman says, "No, but I'll blow you for that toaster over there."

Two students are talking one day in the student union bar.

One says, "Hey, where did you get your new bike from?"

"Well. I was going to a lecture yesterday when a lovely female jumped off the bike, ripped off all her clothes and said, "Come one big boy, you can have anything you want!"

"Right," said his friend, "her clothes wouldn't have fitted you anyway."

A man rushes into his house and yells at his wife, "Sandra, pack your clothes, I've just won the lottery."

Sandra replies, "Shall I pack for warm weather or cold?"

"I don't care," says the man, "just as long as you're out of the here by lunchtime."

A man is driving down Sauchiehall Street when he is flagged down by an attractive hooker.

She says: "I'll do whatever you tell me to for £100."

"OK, " says the man as he hands over the cash. "Paint my flat."

A woman was having trouble with her VW Beetle. She pulled over to the side of the road and opened the hood.

To her amazement, there was nothing there. Another woman in a Beetle stopped to see if she could lend a hand to a fellow Beetle driver.

The first woman said, "Jeez, it seems I don't have an engine in my car!"

The second woman replied "That's OK, I've got a spare one in my boot."

How many sound men does it take to change a lightbulb?

One, two... one, two.

A man and woman are sitting beside each other on a flight to the USA. As the flight takes off, the man sneezes very loudly. Instead of wiping his nose with a hanky, he pulls out his cock and wipes that instead.

The woman can't believe her eyes. She decides to ignore it and hopes it won't happen again.

A few hours later, the man sneezes again. For the second time, he pulls out his prick and gives it another wipe with his hanky. The woman is horrified and says, "Excuse me, but you've sneezed twice in the last few hours and instead of wiping your nose with your hanky, you've pulled out your 'old man' and wiped that instead. What the hell do you think your doing? It's the most disgusting thing I've ever seen."

The man responds by saying, "Oh my. I'm so sorry, I didn't mean to offend you. It's just that everytime I sneeze I have an orgasm. It's a very rare condition. I'm so sorry."

The woman, feeling really bad says, "No, no, It's me who should be sorry. I didn't realise. Please forgive me. Do you take anything for your affliction?"

"Yes," replied the man, "pepper."

**What do you call a basement full of women?
A whine cellar.**

A beautiful blonde woman boards a train to Edinburgh with a ticket for the economy class section. She looks at her seat and then looks into the first-class section. Seeing that the first-class seats appear to be much larger and more comfortable, she moves forward to the last empty one.

The ticket collector checks her ticket and tells the woman that her seat is in economy class. The blonde replies, "I'm young, blonde and beautiful, and I'm going to sit here all the way to Edinburgh."

The ticket collector goes to the driver and informs him of the situation. The driver says that he has a blonde girlfriend and that he can take care of the problem. He goes back and whispers something in the blonde's ear. She immediately gets up, thanks the driver and rushes back to her seat in the economy section. The ticket collector asks the driver how he managed to move the woman. He tells him, "I just told her that the first class section wasn't going to Edinburgh."

A young boy is at a wedding when he asks his dad why the bride wears white.

His dad replies: "Well son, she wears white because it's the happiest day of her life."

The boy then asks his dad why the groom wears black to which the father responds, "Your catching on fast son!"

A male broom and a female broom decided to tie the knot.

The wedding was a beautiful affair. All their friends were there: The mop was looking fantastic, the dustpan and brush wore their best gear and the vacuum cleaner had a tear in its eye as the couple said, 'I do.'

That evening as the couple retired to their Honeymoon cupboard, the female brush said, "I think the two of us will be hearing the swish of little bristles soon. I'm preggers!"

"IMPOSSIBLE!" yelled the male broom. "We haven't even swept together yet!"

Most husbands don't like to hear their wives struggling through the housework, so they turn up the volume on the TV.

How can you tell if a blonde has been using your computer?

There is Tipp-Ex on the screen.

University is like a gorgeous woman?
You try really hard to get in, then nine months later, you wish you had never come.

A prisoner escapes from prison where he had been kept for 15 years.

While running away, he finds a house and breaks into it. He finds a young couple in bed. He gets the guy out of bed, ties him to a chair, then he ties the woman to the bed. While he's on top of her, he kisses her neck, then gets up, and goes to the bathroom.

In his absence, the husband proceeds to tell his wife: "Listen honey, this guy is a prisoner, look at his clothes! He's probably spent a lot of time in prison and hasn't seen a woman in years. I noticed how much he enjoyed kissing your neck. If he wants sex, don't resist, don't complain, just do what he tells you, give him satisfaction. This guy must be dangerous, if he gets angry, he'll kill us. Be strong honey and remember how much I love you."

To which the wife responds: "I am glad you think that way and you're right, he hasn't seen a woman in years, but he wasn't kissing my neck. He was whispering in my ear. He told me that he found you very sexy, and asked if we kept any vaseline in the bathroom. Be strong honey… I love you too!

Sex is like snow: You never know how many inches you're going to get or how long it's going to last.

Angry wife: "What do you mean by coming home half drunk?"

Husband: "It's not my fault. .I ran out of money!"

A woman was talking to her best friend one day.

"Every time my husband climaxes, he lets out a really loud scream."

"Oh, that doesn't sound too bad." replied her friend. "In fact, that would really turn me on!"

"It would turn me on too," replied the woman, "if it didn't keep waking me up!"

A newlywed couple were at home when the woman says to her husband: "I have some fantastic news darling. Pretty soon there is going to be three mouths to feed in this house instead of two."

The husband was so overcome with joy that he grabbed his wife and kissed her passionately.

"I'm so glad you feel this," said his wife, "I didn't think you liked my mother."

A man was complaining to his friend: "I used to have everything I could possibly want - lots of money, a sports car, a huge house and a beautiful woman, then BANG! it was all gone."

"What happened?" asked his friend.

"My wife found out!"

What is the one thing that all men in a singles bar have in common?
  They're all married.

Thee Honeymoon couples are at the same hotel on the first night of their holiday.

  As the first couple are getting undressed, the man says, "Jesus Christ! What a huge arse you've got!"

  The wife isn't too happy about this so she kicks him out of the room.

  The second man says to his wife, "OH MY GOD. What a massive set of thighs you've got!"

  The second wife isn't too pleased about this either so she kicks him out.

  A few minutes later, the third man is kicked out of his room.

  "What happened to you?" the other two men ask him. "Did you put your foot in it?"

  "No," replied the third man, "But I could have!"

"I think bachelors should be heavily taxed." said a married man to his wife. "It's not fair that some men are happier than others."

  My wife has a split personality, and I hate both of them!

One night, while a woman and her husband are making love, she notices he has something stuck in his ear. When she asked him what it was he replied, "For God's sake, will you be quiet woman. I'm trying to listen to the footy."

The doctor came out of the operating theatre with a grave look on his face. "I'm afraid your husband isn't looking too good."

"I don't think so either," replied the woman, "but he's great with the kids."

On the first night of their Honeymoon, a couple were sitting on the edge of the bed.

"Honey, I've never seen a penis before, will you show me what one looks like please?" asked the wife.

The man unzipped his tweeds, got it out and said proudly, "This, my love, is a penis."

"Oh!" she exclaimed, "It looks just like a cock but it's smaller!"

4

Heaven Can Wait

Jokes about religion

Three men were standing in line to get into heaven one day.

It had been a busy day so St Peter had to tell the first one: "Heaven's getting pretty close to full today, and I've been asked to admit only people who have had particularly
horrible deaths. So what's your story?"

The first man replies: "Well, for a while I've suspected my wife has been cheating on me, so today I came home early to try to catch her red-handed.

"As I came into my 25th floor apartment, I could tell something was wrong, but all my searching around didn't reveal where this other guy could have been hiding.

"Finally, I went out to the balcony, and sure enough, there was this man hanging off the railing, 25 floors above ground! By now I was really mad, so I grabbed a hammer and starting hammering on his fingers.

"He let go but even after 25 stories, he fell into the bushes, stunned but okay. I ran into the kitchen, grabbed the fridge and threw it over the edge where it landed on him, killing him instantly.

"But all the stress and anger got to me, and I had a heart attack and died there on the balcony."

"That sounds like a pretty bad day to me," said St Peter, and let the man in.

The second man comes up and Peter explains

to him about heaven being full, and again asks for his story.

"You see, I live on the 26th floor, and every morning I do my exercises out on my balcony. Well, this morning I must have slipped, because I fell over the edge.

"But I got lucky, and caught the railing of the balcony on the floor below me. I knew I couldn't hang on for very long, when suddenly this man burst out onto the balcony. I thought for sure I was saved, but then he started hammering on my fingers.

"Finally I just let go, but I got lucky and fell into the bushes below, stunned but all right. Just when I was thinking I was going to be OK, a refrigerator falls out of the sky and crushes me instantly, and now I'm here."

Once again, St Peter had to concede that that sounded like a pretty horrible death.

The third man came to the front of the line, and again Peter explained that heaven was full and asked for his story.

"Picture this," says the third man, "I'm hiding naked inside a refrigerator..."

What is the definition of innocence?
A nun working in a condom factory thinking she's making sleeping bags for mice.

A guy finds himself in front of the Pearly Gates. St Peter explains that it's not easy to get in heaven. There are some criteria to meet before entry is allowed. For example, was the man religious in life? Attend church? No?...that's bad

Was he generous? give money to the poor? Charities? ...No?...not good

Did he do any good deeds? Help his neighbour? Anything?...NO??

Exasperated, St Peter says ," Look, EVERYBODY does something nice sometimes. Work with me here, I'm trying to help. Now think!"

The man says, "Well, there was this old lady. I came out of a store and found her surrounded by a dozen Hell's Angels. They had taken her purse and were shoving her around. Taunting and abusing her. I got so mad I threw my bags down, fought through the crowd and got her purse back. Helped her to her feet. I then went up to the biggest, baddest biker and told him how despicable, cowardly and mean he was and I spat in his face."

"Wow", said Peter, "That's impressive. When did this happen?"

"Oh, about 10 minutes ago," replied the man.

What's the difference between Jesus and a painting?
It takes only one nail to hang a painting.

Margaret Thatcher died and arrived at the Pearly Gates where St Peter was waiting for her with his clipboard.

"Name?" asked St Peter

"Baroness Thatcher," she replied.

St Peter checked the list and said, "I'm sorry, but you can't come in. Your place is downstairs in Hell."

Thatcher was furious, but turned and started walking down the stairs towards the fiery pit.

Two days later the Devil phoned St Peter and said, "You're gonna have to take that bloody woman back. She's only been here two days and she's closed half of the furnaces already!"

An elderly couple die and arrive at the Pearly Gates. St Peter is there to welcome them. He says, "Over there is your beautiful apartment. It has a swimming pool, a gym, a bar and servants who will take care of your every need. Over on the other side is a fine selection of restaurants serving food from all over the world. Everything is free. If you have any other questions, please, just ask."

The old man turns to his wife and says, "Jeez, if you hadn't put us on that high fibre, skimmed milk diet, we could have been here 15 years ago."

Jesus walks into a hotel, tosses three nails on the front desk and says, "Hey, can you put me up for the night?"

A Catholic, a baptist and a Mormon were bragging about the size of their respective families.

The Catholic said, "I've got four kids. If I had one more I could have a basketball team."

The Baptist said, "I've got ten kids. One more and I could have a football team."

The Mormon said, "That's nothing. I have 17 wives. One more and I could have a golf course."

What is the definition of suspicion?
A nun doing press-ups in a cucumber field.

What do you call a nun who sleepwalks?
A roaming Catholic.

How do you get a nun pregnant?
Dress her up as an atlar boy.

Three nuns are walking down the street when a man jumps out and flashes at them. The first nun has a stroke, the second nun also has a stroke, but the third one didn't touch him.

A priest was walking down the street when a small boy approached from the other direction carrying a bottle of acid. The priest was afraid that the child might injure himself so he offered to trade the bottle of acid for a bottle of holy water.

"What will the Holy water do?" asked the young boy.

"Well," replied the priest, "I rubbed this on a woman's belly and she passed a baby."

The boy replied, "That's nothing. I rubbed this acid on a cat's arse and it passed a motorcycle!"

Two nuns from the Emerald Isle are visiting the USA for the first time. They arrive in New York and the first thing they see is a hotdog stand.

"Blimey O'Reilly," says one nun to the other, "I didn't know they ate dogs in this part of the world. Maybe we should taste one so we fit in with the locals."

So they both buy a hot dog each.

One of the nuns unwraps her dog and stares at it in disbelief.

"Oh sweet jesus, what part of the dog did you get sister?"

Two nuns were on a day trip to Edinburgh Zoo. As they passed the gorilla enclosure, they saw one of the male gorillas howling and beating his chest in sexual desire. Before they knew what was happening, the gorilla had leapt over the enclosure wall and had begun ravishing one of the nuns. When it had finished, it leapt back over the wall and back into his hiding place.

The nun, got up off the floor, dusted herself off and said to the other nun, "No matter what happens, please don't tell ANYONE about this."

The other nun agreed and they continued on their way.

Several years later, the nuns meet again in a park.

"I'm sorry to bring the whole episode up again, but can I ask you a question about that day in the Zoo?" asked the nun.

"If you must," replied the other.

"Well, did it hurt?" asked the nun.

"Did it hurt?" replied the nun, "Of course it bloody hurt. He never called, he never wrote or sent a box of chocolates."

What do you get when you cross a devil
worshipper and a jehovah's witness?
Someone who goes from door to door
telling people to go to hell.

There are two Glasgow ministers who ride their bikes to work every morning.

One sunny morning, one of the ministers arrives at work without his bike.

"What happened to your bike?" asks the first minister.

"Well," says the other, "I woke up this morning and I couldn't find it anywhere."

The other minister says, "At your next sermon, mention the Ten Commandments and when you get to 'Thou Shalt Not Steal' the culprit will surely come forward and return the bike.

The two met up again the next week, and lo and behold, the minister was riding his bike again.

"Well, well, well, I see my advice about the Ten Commandments worked."

"It sure did," said the minister, "When I was reading the Ten Commandments, I got to 'Thou Shalt Not Commit Adultery' when I suddenly remembered where I'd left it!"

A mum walked into the bathroom one day only to find her son scrubbing his private parts with a toothbrush and toothpaste.

"Sweet Jesus of Nazareth!" exclaimed the mother, "What the Hell do you think you're doing?"

"Don't try and stop me, mum. I'm doing this five times a day, because if you think I'm going to end up with a cavity that looks as bad as my big sisters you've got another thing coming!"

Why were most of Jesus' apostles fishermen and not cabinet makers?
If they had been cabinet makers, Jesus would have to have said: "Drop your drawers and follow me!"

A drunken old man wanders into his local church and makes his way to the confessionals. He sits there in silence. The priest coughs to get the drunks attention, but the man ignores him and continues to sit in silence.

The priest waits another minute before coughing again, this time a wee bit louder. The drunk continues to ignore the priest.

The priest then knocks on the partition in a final attempt to get the man's attention.

"It's no bloody use knocking," says the man, "There's no toilet paper in here either."

A guy walks into a confession booth. "Forgive me father for I have sinned," he says, "I almost had an affair with a woman."

The priest is slightly bemused by this and asks the man, "Almost? Tell me more my son."

"Well," says the man, "I met this girl and we rubbed up against each other for a bit before we both came to our senses and realised what we were about to do was wrong." said the man.

"Well my son," says the priest, "Rubbing against is just as sinful as putting it in. You must never approach this woman again and you must put £20 in the donation box."

The man begins to walk out of the church without dropping any money into the box.

"Hey, you there!" shouts the priest, "I saw that, you didn't put £20 in the box."

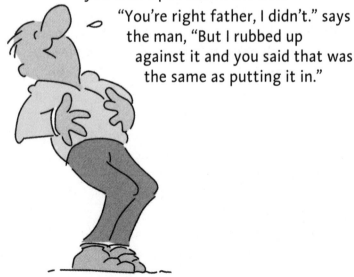

"You're right father, I didn't." says the man, "But I rubbed up against it and you said that was the same as putting it in."

Ex-USA President Bill Clinton dies and finds himself at the gates of Hell. Satan tells Bill he has a choice of where he spends the rest of eternity.

He leads Bill into door No.1. Inside, there is a man standing in a pot of molten lava with people throwing hot coals at his head.

"What do you think Bill?" says Satan.

"No chance, that would hurt to much." says Bill.

Inside door No.2, there is a guy on a spit being slowly roasted over the fires of Hell.

"What about this eternity?" says Satan.

"You've got to be joking me." says Bill.

Satan then opens up door No.3.

Inside, a man is tied naked to a post and kneeling in front of him Monica Lewinsky is giving him a blow job.

"Whooohooo," exclaims Bill, "Now this I can handle!"

"Ah, a fine choice Bill," says Satan, "Monica - you can go now."

5

Down The Boozer

Jokes about life in the pub

A young man was sitting at a bar enjoying a refreshment or two, when an attractive buxom blonde approached him and suggested they had a drink together.

"Alright then", said the young man, "I'm no millionaire, but I'll buy a couple of drinks."

After the drink, the young blonde suggested they had a dance.

The young man smiled and said, "I'm no Fred Astaire, but I'll give it a whirl."

Later that evening, the woman suggested they go back to her flat.

The young man laughed and said, "I'm no Cary Grant but I'll follow you up there."

After they had done the deed the woman said, "What about some cash?"

To which the young man replied, "I ain't no gigolo, but I'll take it."

A red indian walks into a saloon dressed as a cowboy. He says, "Me wantum beer!"

He drinks the beer, goes to the bathroom, pulls out a rifle, shoots the toilet, grabs his bag, pulls out a cat and takes a huge bite out of it.

"Jeez," said the landlord, "What the hell are you doing?"

The indian replies, "Me like playing white man. Me drink beer, shoot da shit and eat pussy."

A group of guys were having a few scoops after work one day when a stunning lass walks in and sits down in the middle of them.

"Don't you recognise me guys? It's me Dennis. I've had a sex change!"

All the guys were amazed at how good he looked with all his new bits.

One of the guys asked: "Tell me mate, what was the most painful part of the operation? Was it when they cut off your love length?"

"No. That was painful, but it wasn't the most painful thing." replied Dennis.

Another guy says, "I bet I know what the most painful thing was. It must have been when they lopped off yer baws?"

"No, that hurt, but the most painful part of the operation was when they cut out half of my brain."

Two friends are out for a couple of pints. After a few refreshments they both rush off to the toilet to take a slash.

One of the guys, Shugg, notices that his mate Scott is pretty well endowed and decides to ask him what his secret is.

"Well," says Scott: "It wasn't always this size, I can tell you."

"I visited a specialist who said he could make me more of a man with a small operation. But he said it would cost £15,000."

"If you like," said Scott, "I'll give you the name of the specialist if you're interested?"

"Too right mate," said Shugg.

A couple of months later, the lads meet up again in the bogs of their local boozer.

"Did you give the specialist a call?" asked Scott

"Take a look for yourself," boasted Shugg with a wry smile.

"What do ya think of that then?' he asked. "It only cost me £5000"

Scott shrugged and said, "You've been done mate. No wonder it only cost £5000. They've given you my old one."

An Irishman walks into a bar in Dublin, orders three pints of Guinness and sits in the back of the room, drinking each one in turn.

When he finishes, he orders three more. The barman approaches and says, "It might taste better if you bought one at a time."

The Irishman replies, "Well, you see, I have two brothers. One is in America, the other is in Australia. When we all left home, we promised that we would drink this way to remember the days when we all drank together. So I have one for each o' me brothers and one for me self."

The barman admits that this is a nice custom, and leaves it there.

The Irishman becomes a regular, and always drinks the same way.

One day, he comes in and orders two pints.

All the regulars take notice and fall silent. When he comes back to the bar for the second round, the barman says, "I don't want to intrude on your grief, but I wanted to offer my condolences on your recent loss."

The Irishman says, "Oh, no. Everyone's fine," he explains, "It's just that my doctor told me to stop drinking."

Rick Waller and his brother walk into a pub. Rick says to his brother, "Your round."

His bother replies, "So are you, you fat b***d!"**

Tom and Bob fancied a pint or two but didn't have a lot of money, altogether they had a staggering 50 pence. Tom said: "Hang on, I've an idea." He went into the butchers shop next door and came out with one large Cumberland sausage.

Bob: "Are you crazy? Now we haven't got any money left at all." Tom said: "Don't worry, just follow me."

They went into a pub where he immediately ordered two pints and two large Jack Daniels'

Bob said: "Now you've blown it. Do you know how much trouble we will be in? We haven't got any money!"

Tom replied: "Don't worry, I've got a plan"

They had their drinks and Tom said, "OK, I'll stick the sausage through my zip, you get on your knees and put it in your mouth."

Said and done, the landlord noticed, went berserk and threw them out.

They continued this, pub after pub, getting more and more drunk – all for free. At the 10th pub Bob said: "Listen mate - I don't think I can continue this any longer. I'm pissed and my knees are killing me"

Tom replied: "How do you think I feel, I lost the sausage two hours ago!"

A skeleton walks into a pub, grabs a stool and orders a beer.
  "Anything else?," asked the barman.
  The says, "Yeah...a mop..."

A guy walks into a bar and sees a lot of people crowded around a table. Curious, the man pushes his way to the front of the crowd to see what the commotion is about.

On the table is an upside down pot with a small duck tap dancing on it.

"Wow!" exclaims the guy, "How much do you want for it?"

"Well, I can let you have it for £2000" says the duck owner.

The guy hands over the cash and takes the duck home.

The next day, the guy turns back up at the pub in a furious rage.

"Hey, you've ripped me off!" he screams. "I got the duck home and it hasn't danced once. I demand my money back!" he screamed.

The guy who sold the duck looks somewhat unimpressed and says: "Did you remember to light the candle under the pot?"

What's the difference between a Dundonian swampdonkey and a Dundonian goddess?
  About five pints.

A guy is having a drink in his local when he leans over to a woman next to him and says: "Do you want to hear a really good blonde joke?"

She replies: "Well, before you tell that joke, you should know that I'm blonde, 6ft 4ins, 16 stone and a bodybuilder.

"The blonde woman sitting next to me is 6ft 5ins and a professional weightlifter. The woman beside her is also a blonde who is a kickboxing champ who could whip your ass in a second. Do you still want to tell that blonde joke?"

"Nah, not if I'm going to have to explain it three times!"

A guy skipped into his local one day with a huge smile on his face.

The barman looked at him and said: "Why are you so happy today then Dave?"

"My wife has just run off with my best friend." he replied.

"Really, why are you so happy then," asked the barman.

"They have saved me a lot of money," replied the guy, they were both pregnant!"

A guy leaves his local boozer early so he wouldn't be in trouble with his wife. When he arrived home, he discovers his wife in bed with her boss. Back at the pub later the barman says: "That's terrible, what did you do?"

"Well," says the guy, "I crept out of the house and ran down here. They were just getting started, so I reckon I've got time for a couple more beers!"

A drunk gets on a bus, staggers up the aisle and sits next to an old lady, breathing fumes all over her. She stares at the man with contempt and says: "I've got news for you mister. You're going straight to Hell."

The drunk jumps out of his seat and shouts, "Christ, I'm on the wrong bleedin' bus!"

A guy walks into his local and orders a glass of cola.

"Cola," replies the barman, "You always have beer when you're here. Why the change?"

"Well," says the guy, "last night I staggered home in a right state and blew chunks, so I'm not feeling to well today."

"Awww, come on, that happens to us all at some point. Don't worry about it."

"No, no," replies the guy, "You don't understand. Chunks is my dog."

So this dyslexic walks into a bra...

A piece of road comes barging into a pub shouting abuse, screaming and demanding a pint from the barman.

Two off-duty police officers are having a quiet pint and are keeping a close eye on the angry piece of road.

The road then starts to smash some of the glasses on the bar and starts swearing loudly.

One of the police officers decides that enough is enough and gets up to have a word with the road.

His colleague grabs his arm and says: "Just be careful Steve, watch out, he's a well known cycle path

A drunken bum collapsed on the corner of a street. A policeman sees that the man is in some distress and approaches him to see if he can help.

The drunk says: "Don't worry aboot me pal, I know the world rotates every 24 oors, so am waitin' for ma hoose tae come by. I don't hink it wull be lang noo 'cos ah jist saw ma neighbour passin' a wee while ago!"

This day of the year always brings back a lot of sad memories for me. It was two years ago that I lost my wife, my children and my home. I'll never forget that poker game down the pub.

A guy is sitting in a strange boozer when he gets an urge to go for a slash. He doesn't like the look of any of the locals in the pub and is a bit wary of leaving his pint. He decides to write a note on a cigarette paper and sticks it to the side of his beer. It says: "I've spat in this pint, so don't touch it."

When he arrives back to his beer, there is another cigarette paper attached to the glass which reads: "So did we!"

A guy picks up a girl in a bar and they go back to his hotel room.

After making love, he asks her, "Am I the first guy you've ever made love to?"

"You could be," she replies, "Your face looks familiar."

An old couple were on holiday in the Lake District. They stopped at a small pub for a bit of lunch which they really enjoyed.

After they had been driving for half an hour, the old woman realised that she had left her glasses at the table of the pub.

The old man was forced to turn the car around and he wasn't happy about it. In fact he complained all the way back to the pub.

When the old woman was clambering out of the car he said, "While you're in there, you may as well get my hat. It should be on the table next to your glasses."

6

Sporting Life

Jokes about the world of sport

HER SIDE OF THE STORY:
"He was in an odd mood when I got to the bar tonight. I thought it might have been my fault because I was a bit late, but he didn't say anything about it.

I don't remember doing anything to make him upset, but I could tell there was something wrong.

We went to the restaurant and he was STILL acting a bit funny. I was getting really worried, what did I do? I tried to cheer him up, but it didn't work. I asked him if he was upset with me, and he said no. But I'm not really sure. I told him that I loved him and he just put his arm around me!

We finally got back to his place and I was wondering if he was going to break up with me. Why didn't he want to talk about it? I tried to ask him about it, but he just switched on the TV. I went to bed upset. After ten minutes, he came into the bedroom and we had sex. I thought that maybe he would open up after we shared some intimacy, but he still seemed really distracted. I just cried myself to sleep. He didn't even notice how upset I was! I'm so confused, I think he might have met someone else?"

HIS SIDE OF THE STORY:
Played like shit today - shot 83 - can't putt. Felt kind of tired all day.

Got laid though!

On a tour of Scotland, the Pope took a couple of days off his itinerary to visit the North coast near Aberdeen on an sightseeing trip.

The Popemobile was driving along the golden sands when they heard a commotion up ahead. Upon approaching the scene the Pope noticed just outside the surf, a hapless man wearing an England jersey, struggling frantically to free himself from the jaws of a twenty foot shark.

At that moment a speedboat containing three men wearing Scotland football tops roared into view from around the point. Spontaneously, one of the men took aim and fired a harpoon into the shark's ribs, immobilising it instantly.

The other two reached out and pulled the Englishman from the water and then, using long clubs, beat the shark to death.

They bundled the bleeding, semi conscious man into the speed boat along with the dead shark and then prepared for a hasty retreat, when they heard frantic shouting from the shore. It was of course the Pope, and he summoned them to the beach.

Upon them reaching the shore the Pope went into raptures about the rescue and said, "I give you my blessing for your brave actions. I had heard that there were some racist xenophobic people trying to divide Scotland and England, but, now I have seen with my own eyes this is not true. I can see that your society is a truly enlightened example of racial harmony and could serve as a model on which other nations could follow."

He blessed them all and drove off in a cloud of dust.

As he departed, the harpoonist asked the others, "Who was that?"

"That," one answered, "was his Holiness the Pope. He is in direct contact with God and has access to all God's wisdom."

"Well," the harpoonist replied, "he knows nothing about shark hunting. By the way, how's the bait holding up or do we need to get another one?"

The psychology instructor had just finished a lecture on mental health and was giving an oral test.

Speaking specifically about manic depression, she asked, "How would you diagnose a patient who walks back and forth screaming at the top of his lungs one minute, then sits in a chair weeping uncontrollably the next?"

A young man in the rear raised his hand and answered, "A football manager?"

A man goes to a confessional. "Forgive me father, for I have sinned."

"What is your sin, my child?" the priest asks.

"Well," the man starts, "I used some horrible language this week and I feel absolutely terrible."

"When did you use this awful language?" asked the priest.

"I was golfing and hit an incredible drive that looked like it was going to go over 260 yards, but it struck a phone line and fell straight down to the ground after going only about 100 yards."

"Is that when you swore?"

"No, Father," said the man. "After that, a squirrel ran out of the bushes and grabbed my ball in his mouth and ran away."

"Is THAT when you swore?" asked the priest.

"No," said the man, "You see, as the squirrel was running away, a crow grabbed it in it's beak and began to fly away!"

"Is THAT when you swore?" asked the amazed priest.

"No, not yet." The man replied. "As the crow carried the squirrel away, it flew towards the green. As it passed over the trees, the squirrel dropped the ball."

"Did you swear THEN?" asked the now impatient priest.

"No, because as the ball fell it struck a tree, bounced off a big rock, and rolled onto the green and stopped within six inches of the hole."

"You missed the bloody putt, didn't you?" sighed the priest.

A man and his wife are out golfing. They have had a great time and the man has had a near perfect game. The final hole, the most difficult, wraps around an old barn. With a terrible slice, the man puts the barn between his ball and the green.

Knowing that this will destroy his score, he begins to rant and rave. His wife makes a suggestion.

"What if I were to hold open the barn doors? That way you could send the ball right through the barn and onto the green."

He thinks it over and decides that it will work. With his wife holding open the barn door he lines up with the hole and gives the ball a terrific 'whack!' The ball shoots through the air and right into the head of his wife, killing her instantly.

Months go by, the man mourning all the while. His friends, hating to see him in such a state, convince him to go golfing with them. They end up at the same course and on the final hole, another terrible slice puts the old barn between his ball and the green. Again he begins to rant and rave. His friend, wanting to please him, makes a suggestion.

"What if I were to hold open the barn doors? That way you could send it right through the barn onto the green."

"No," the man replies, "last time I did that I got two over par."

There once were two best friends named Joe and Rab. They were two of the biggest football fans in Scotland. Their entire lives revolved around football. Joe and Rab discussed the history of football and they examined every score during the season. They went to over 50 games a year. They even agreed that whoever died first would try to come back and tell the other if there was football in heaven.

One summer night, Joe passed away in his sleep after watching the European Cup final earlier in the evening. He died a happy man.

A few nights later, his mate Rab awoke to the sound of Joe's voice from beyond.

"Joe is that you?" Rab asked.

"Of course it me," Joe replied.

"This is unbelievable!" Rab exclaimed. "So tell me, is there football in heaven?"

"Well, I have some good news and some bad

news for you. Which do you want to hear first?"

"Tell me the good news first."

"Well, the good news is that there is football in heaven, Rab."

"Oh, that's wonderful! So what could possibly be the bad news?"

"You're on the squad list for tomorrow night."

The National Science Foundation announced the following study results on UK business recreation preferences:

1. Sport of choice for maintenance level employees: BOWLING

2. Sport of choice for front line workers: FOOTBALL

3. Sport of choice for supervisors: BASEBALL

4. Sport of choice for middle management: TENNIS

5. Sport of choice for corporate chairmen: GOLF

CONCLUSION: The higher you are in the corporate structure, the smaller your balls.

The manager of Airdrie Utd was woken up by a call from his local police station. "I'm afraid that the stadium has been broken into."

Horrified, the manager asked, "Did they get the cups?"

"No sir," the policeman replied, "They didn't get into the kitchen."

The real reason men like to go fishing is that it's the only time anyone will ever say to them, "Oh my God, that's a huge one!"

Alex and Ryan are out for a round of golf when Alex hits his ball into a bunker. As they approach, Alex spots a beautiful woman having a crap in the bunker.

He grabs Ryan and they both hide behind a nearby tree while they have a look.

"This is incredible. A beautiful woman like that actually relieving herself in the woods." says Ryan.

"Yeah," says Alex, "I bet she won't even wipe her arse when she's finished."

Ryan is shocked. "No way! A beautiful woman like that would never be so disgusting."

Alex replies, "I'm telling you she won't wipe and I'm so confident, that I'll bet you £10."

"You're on!" said Ryan.

Suddenly Alex stepped out from behind the tree and shouted: "Hey, what do you think you're doing?"

There was a nasty no good biker riding his Harley down a B road in Fife, when he spotted a cat lying in the middle of the road. The biker thought to himself: "I'll cut that cat in two," and he bore down on it hard.

As he got closer, though, he suddenly realised that it was not a cat, but a large piece of metal lying in the road. Too late! His front wheel plowed into it and he was sent flying over the handlebars and onto the road at 110 MPH.

When he arrived in Hell, the Devil shook the ex-biker's hand, he asked mockingly: "So, how do you like it here?"

The bad-ass biker replied, "Man, this is one COOL place!"

The old Devil was just a little miffed at this, so he decided to crank up the thermostat a notch. The next day, the Devil sought out the biker and asked, "So, how do you like it now?"

The biker responded by saying, "This is great! Reminds me of a drug run I did down in Spain."

Naturally, the Devil was only more angered, and cranked the heat up as far as it could go. The next day the Devil again found the biker, and asked how he was holding up.

Undaunted, the biker proclaimed, "It's almost as hot as the time I beat up and robbed two holidaymakers down in the Med"

By now the Devil was furious, so he turned the thermostat all the way down.

The next morning, he tracked down the biker

again and asked, "OK smart-ass, how do you like it NOW?"

With icicles hanging from every part of his body, the biker shivered and chattered, "W-w-w-what h-h-happened, d-d-d-did Partick Thistle f-f-finally w-w-win the league?"

What's the difference between Motherwell FC and a triangle?
  A triangle's got three points.

Two blokes are out on the golf course one fine day when one of them turns to the other and says, "Did you here about David Ure? He went mad last weekend and beat his wife to death with a golf club.

"Oh my God, that's terrible!" said the other golfer.

They paused for a moment before the other said, "How many strokes did it take him?"

Why doesn't Mexico have an Olympic team?
  Because everyone who can run, jump and swim is already in the USA.

Near the end of a particularly trying round of golf, during which the golfer had hit numerous bad shots, he said in frustration to his caddy: "I'd move heaven and earth to break a hundred on this course."

"Why don't you try Heaven," said the caddy. "You've already moved most of the Earth."

Some years ago, a sultan who had six children, all girls, began to despair as he had no son and heir. Imagine his joy when one of his wives finally presented him with a son and heir.

Just before his son's sixth birthday, the Sultan took him to one side and said: "Son, I am very proud of you. Anything you want, I shall get for you."

His son replied: "Daddy, I would like to have my own plane."

Not wanting to do anything by halves, his father bought him American Airlines.

Just before his son's seventh birthday, the Sultan took him to one side. "Son, you are my pride and joy. Anything you want, I shall get for you.

"His son replied: "Daddy, I would like a boat." Not wanting to do anything halfway, his father bought him The Princess Cruise Line.

Just before his son's eighth birthday, the Sultan took him to one side.

"Son, you bring so much happiness to my life.

Anything you want, I shall get for you."

His son replied, "Daddy, I would like to be able to watch cartoons." Not wanting to look a cheapskate, his father bought him Disney Studios and their theatres, where he watched all his favourite cartoons.

Just before his son's ninth birthday, the Sultan took him to one side. "Son, you are an inspiration to us all. Anything you want, I shall get for you."

His son, who was by now really into the Disney cartoons, replied, "Daddy, I would like a Mickey Mouse outfit."

Not wanting to appear to be tight, his father bought him Dundee United.

Three guys were on a skiing holiday and they had to stay in the same room and more importantly, the same bed on their first night because nothing else was available.

The next morning, the guy who slept on the right hand side of the bed said: "Last night I had a really strange dream that I was masturbating furiously but I couldn't feel my hands!"

"That's really strange." replied the guy who slept on the left hand side of the bed, "I had the same dream!"

"God, you guys are crazy!" said the guy who had slept in the middle. "I dreamt I was skiing!"

Fast forward to 2006 - it is just before Scotland v Brazil at the next World Cup Group game. Ronaldo goes into the Brazilian changing room to find all his team mates looking a bit glum.

"What's up?" he asks.

"Well, we're having trouble getting motivated for this game. We know it's important but it's only Scotland. They're shite and we can't be arsed".

Ronaldo looks at them and says "Well, I reckon I can beat this by myself, you lads go down the pub."

So Ronaldo goes out to play Scotland by himself and the rest of the Brazilian team go off for a few jars.

After a few pints they wonder how the game is going, so they get the landlord to put the teletext on.

A big cheer goes up as the screen reads "Brazil 1 - Scotland 0 (Ronaldo 10minutes)". He is beating Scotland all by himself!

Anyway, a few more pints later and the game is forgotten until someone remembers "It must be full time now, let's see how he got on". They put the teletext on.

"Result from the Stadium "Brazil 1(Ronaldo 10 minutes) - Scotland 1(Stephen Thompson 89minutes)".

They can't believe it, he has single handedly got a draw against Scotland!!

They rush back to the Stadium to congratulate

him. They find him in the dressing room, still in his gear, sitting with his head in his hands.

He refuses to look at them. "I've let you down, I've let you down."

"Don't be daft, you got a draw against Scotland , all by yourself. And they only scored at the very very end!"

"No, No, I have, I've let you down... I got sent off after 12 minutes"

Why did God invent Golf?
So men had an excuse to dress up like pimps.

Two guys are getting changed after a game of footy when one of the lads notices the other guy has a large cork up his arse.

"Jesus wept mate, how the hell did that happen?"

"Well, when I was on holiday in Spain, I was taking a stroll along the beach with my missus, when I tripped over a rock and landed on a bottle. I gave the bottle a quick rub and, POOF, out popped a genie! The genie said he would grant me one wish, and one wish only, so I said, 'No shit!"

A guy was walking his three legged greyhound in the park one morning, when he noticed something shining in the undergrowth.

He stooped down to investigate further and realised it was a magic lamp.

He began rubbing the lamp and, sure enough, out popped a genie.

"Oh my," exclaimed the guy, "If you could make it possible for my three-legged greyhound to win a few races, I could put my life savings on it and I would be sure to be a wealthy man. No-one would give me good odds on this thing winning anything!"

"Mmmmm," pondered the genie, "That goes against rule 461 of the genie wish guide rulebook. That would be an obvious sign of divine intervention and is frowned upon by my bosses. Maybe I can sort something else out for you?"

"Well, I suppose you could," replied the man, "You see, I'm a big fan of Kilmarnock FC, so if you could arrange for them to win the SPL this season, that would be fantastic!"

The genie sighed. "About that dog of yours..."

"I have a confession," a guy said to his new wife. "I am golf crazy. I can't get enough of it and I spend all my weekends playing golf with my friends. So you won't see that much of me during the weekend."

"That's OK honey," replied the wife, "I'm a hooker."

"No problem!" exclaimed the guy. "Just keep your head down and straighten your left arm."

A man goes skydiving for the first time. After listening to the instructor for what seems like days, he is ready to go. Excited, he jumps out of the airplane. After a bit, he pulls the ripcord.

Nothing happens.

He tries again.

Still nothing.

He starts to panic, but remembers his back-up chute. He pulls that cord.

Nothing happens.

He frantically begins pulling both cords, but to no avail. Suddenly, he looks down and he can't believe his eyes. Another man is in the air with him, but this guy is going up!

Just as the other guy passes by, the skydiver - who by this time scared out of his wits - yells "Hey, do you know anything about skydiving?"

The other guy yells back, "No! Do you know anything about gas cookers?"

A guy walks into a bar in Edinburgh with a rare jet black dachshund under his arm. The dog is kitted out entirely in maroon and has a maroon patch over his right eye.

"Could you turn on the TV please, mate?" the customer asks the barman.

"My little friend here's a mad one-eyed Hearts supporter and he wants to see tonight's match against Dundee."

The guy orders a pint and pours some into an ashtray for his football mad maroon clad canine.

During the first half, Mark De Vries scores from a free-kick and the maroon clad dog goes ballistic.

It starts howling, turning cartwheels, punching holes in the stratosphere and executing precision pelvic thrusts.

The dogs excited behaviour continues well into the second half.

"Jesus," says the barman. "That's awesome! What did he do when they won the league?"

"Dunno," says the customer. "I've only had him twenty years..."

7

Time For
A Quicky

**A collection of jokes that are
straight to the point**

What do you give a man who has everything?
A woman to show him how to work it.

How does a man show he's been planning for the future?
He buys two crates of beer instead of one.

What's the difference between a new husband and a new dog?
After a year, the dog is still pleased to see you.

How do you save a dog from drowning?
Take your foot off it's head.

What do men and beer bottles have in common?
They're both empty from the neck up?

How many men does it take to change a roll of toilet paper?
We don't know, It's never happened.

How do you make a hormone?
Don't pay her.

What do you get when you cross PMT with ESP?
A bitch who thinks she knows everything.

What are the three words you don't want to hear while making love?
Honey, I'm home.

What's the difference between hard and light?
You can sleep with a light on.

What's pink and hard in the morning?
The Financial Times crossword.

What do you get when you cross a nun with a PC?
A computer that never goes down on you.

Why is it good to have Alzheimer's Disease?
You can hide your own Easter eggs.

How do you get a one armed Irishman out of a tree?
Wave at him.

What is the difference between yogurt and Australia?
Yogurt has a real live culture.

What lies at the bottom of the sea and whimpers?
A nervous wreck.

What is a computer's first sign of old age?
Loss of memory

What happened to the computer who fell on the floor?
It slipped a disc

WARNING: There is a new computer virus doing the rounds called Viagra. It turns your 3.5 inch floppy into a hard drive!

What did the sign on the door of the brothel say?
Beat it. Cos we're closed.

Why is air like sex?
Because it's no big deal until you're not getting
any.

What is another name for pickled bread?
Dill-dough.

What do you do with 365 used condoms?
Melt them down, make a car tyre and call it a
Goodyear.

Why is a woman like a laxative?
They both irritate the shit out of you.

What's worse than a male chauvinist?
A woman who won't do what she's told.

Why do women rub their eyes when they wake up?
Because they don't have balls to scratch.

What do you call a virgin in a swimming pool?
A cherry float.

What is the difference between your wife and your job?
After five years your job will still suck.

Why don't women need to wear watches?
There's a clock on the oven.

What's six inches long, two inches wide and drives women wild?
Cash

Why did the woman cross the road?
Who cares? How did she get out of the kitchen?

How many women does it take to change a bulb?
Who cares? Let her cook in the dark!

What's the difference between your wife and a wheelie bin?
You only need to take a wheelie bin out once a week.

Why are women's feet so small?
So they can stand closer to the sink.

Have you heard about the new super-sensitive condoms you can buy?
They hang around after sex and talk to the woman after you've rolled over and gone to sleep.

Why haven't we sent a woman to the moon yet?
It doesn't need cleaning.

What do prostitutes and bungee-jumping have in common?
They both cost too much money and if the rubber snaps you're buggered.

If your dog is barking at the back door trying to get in and your wife is at the front door trying to get in, who do you let in first?
The dog. At least when he's in he shuts up.

How do you turn a fox into an elephant?
Marry it.

What's better than roses on your piano?
Tulips on your organ.

What do you do if your dishwasher stops working?
Shout at her.

What do you do if you're girlfriend starts to smoke?
Slow down and lubricate.

What is it when a man talks dirty to a woman?
Sexual Harassment
And what is it if a woman talks dirty to a man?
£2 a minute.

How many men does it take to open a beer bottle?
None, it should be open when she gives it to you!

What is the difference between a man buying a
lottery ticket and a man arguing with his wife?
The man buying the lottery ticket has more chance
of winning.

What is the difference between a bachelor and a
married man?
A bachelor comes home, sees what's in the fridge
and goes to bed. A married man comes home, sees
what's in the bed and goes to the fridge.

Why do female black widow spiders kill their partners after mating?
To stop the snoring before it starts.

What does it take for a man to plan a candlelit dinner?
A power failure

Why is sleeping with a man like a soap opera?
Just when it's getting interesting, it's all over until next time.

What do theme parks and Viagra have in common?
They both make you wait hours for a two-minute ride.

What did the elephant say to the naked man?
I can't believe you breathe through a thing that small.

Why don't guys give their penises female names?
Because they don't want a woman running their life.

What's the difference between ET and a man?
ET phoned home.

Why don't little girls fart?
Because they don't get arseholes until they are
married.

Why can't women read maps?
Because only blokes can comprehend the concept
of an inch equalling a mile.

What two words clear out a men's changing room
quickest?
Nice cock!

What is the sex speed limit?
68, because when you get to 69 you have to turn around.

What is the difference between a snowgirl and a snowman?
Snowballs.

What happens when you kiss a canary?
You get chirpes and it can't be tweeted because it's a canarial disease.

What has two grey legs and two brown legs?
An elephant with diarrhoea.

Did you hear they just found a new use for sheep in Aberdeen?
Making wool.

What happened to the Pope when he went to Mount Olive?
Popeye nearly killed him.

What is "egghead?"
What Mrs Dumpty gives to Humpty.

What is the noisiest thing in the whole world?
Skeletons shagging on a tin roof.

What do you call a young rabbit?
A pubic hare.

Have you heard the one about the blind circumciser?
He got the sack.

How do you know if you have acne?
Blind people can read your face.

What do you call a nun who has had a sex changer?
A tran-sister.

What is brown, smelly and sits on a piano stool?
Beethoven's First Movement.

What is gross about a lung transplant?
The first time you cough after the operation, it's not your phlegm!

What happens when you cross a male chicken and a flea?
You get an itchy cock.

What's black, sits by a bed and takes the piss out of you?
A dialysis machine.

Why did the man put all of his money in the freezer?
He wanted some cold, hard cash.

What's brown and sticky?
A stick!

How do you know that carrots are good for your eyesight?
Well, have you ever seen a rabbit wearing glasses?

What do you call a surgeon with 8 arms?
A doctopus

Why do men prefer to take showers rather than baths?
Pissing in the bath is revolting.

What do you call kids born in whorehouses?
Brothel sprouts.

Why did the one-handed man cross the road?
To get to the second hand-shop

What's the difference between a tampon and a cowboy hat?
Cowboy hats are for arseholes.

Which meat is cheapest in the USA?
Deer balls. You'll find them under a buck.

Have you heard about the constipated maths teacher?
He worked it out with a pencil.

Why don't skeletons fight each other?
They don't have the guts.

What did the alien say when he landed in the Botanic Gardens?
Take me to your weeder.

What do you call something that's 12 inches long and hangs in front of an arsehole?
A politicians tie.

How will we remember Big Bill Clinton?
The President after Bush!

What do politicians and nappies have in common?
The both need to be changed on a regular basis and are both full of shit.

What are MP's like self amusers?
They are both mass-debaters.

**What do you call a condom running down a
window?
Condomation.**

What is green and pecks on trees?
Woody Wood Pickle.

**Why is a whore like a door knob?
Because everyone gets a turn.**

How can you spot a woman wearing tights?
Her ankles swell when she farts.

**What's the difference between a blonde and a
cockerel?
The cockerel says, "Cock-a-doodle-doo", while the
blonde says, "Any cock'll-do."**

How many nuclear scientists does it take to change a lightbulb?
None, they glow in the dark.

Why don't whores vote at General Elections?
They don't care who gets in as long as someone loses their deposit.

A cowboy walks into a bar, dressed in a paper suit.
It wasn't long before the sherrif arrested him for rustling.

What is a 72?
A 69 with three people watching.

Why is a degree like a condom?
It's rolled up when you get it, it represents a lot of effort and it's worthless the next day.

How does Michael Jackson pick his nose?
By catalogue.

8

Pic n' mix

A selection of quality jokes

Sean and Paddy landed themselves jobs in the local sawmill. Just before lunch, Paddy yelled, "Mick! I've lost me bleeding finger!"

"Oh have you," replied Sean. "And how did you manage that?"

"I just touched this big spinning thing here like this. Shit… There goes another one!"

"Hello, is that American Airlines?" said Big Mick McClaferty. "Could you tell me how long it takes to fly from Dublin to Boston?"

The girl on the other end of the phone said, "I'll see sir, Just a minute."

"Ah, 'tis fast to be sure. Thank ye," Mick said as he hung up."

Little Johnny was sitting in class one day when he suddenly wanted to go to the toilet. He yelled out, "Excuse me Miss Duff, I really need to take a piss."

"Now, now Johnny, that is not the proper word to use. If you need to go to the toilet, please use the word 'urinate.'

Little Johnny thinks about this for a moment and says, "You're an eight, but if you had bigger tits you'd be a ten."

A man started a job in a pickle factory, but after a week he had to visit his psychiatrist.

"I've got to leave the pickle factory," he said, "every time I start work I have a burning desire to put my cock into the pickle slicer."

The psychiatrist told him to relax and go back to work and see how things went.

After another week the man visited the quack again. This time he was even worse.

Again the shrink told him to fight the urge and calm down.

The next week the man cane back and said to the shrink, "Well, I finally did it. I put my shlong in the pickle slicer."

"Good God man, are you alright?"

"The boss came in and caught me and I got the sack."

"What about the pickle slicer?" asked the shrink.

"She got the sack as well."

Jimmy, did your mother help you with your homework last night?" the teacher asked.
"No, she did it all by herself."

A mute was walking through town one day when he met an old friend who was also couldn't speak.

In sign language he asked his old pal how he was keeping. His friend spoke to him.

"Jesus, why don't you stop all that handwaving shit. I can talk now." he said.

Astonished, the mute asked how this was possible.

The guy responded by saying that he had gone to a specialist doctor who had cured him of his affliction.

Gesturing wildly, the mute asked for the doctors phone number so he could make an appointment.

The next day, the mute visited the doctors surgery.

The doc told the mute that he had exactly the same symptoms as his friend and that it should be no problem to cure.

The doctor told the mute to drop his trousers and to bend over the examination table.

The guy did as he was told. The doctor then produced a long pole and a jar of vaseline.

The doctor then shoved the long pole up the guys ass.

"AAAAAAaaaaaaaaaaaaaa" screamed the mute.

"Very good," said the doctor. "Next week we'll move on to the letter B."

As part of a funeral package, an undertaker agreed to provide a six word funeral notice in the local paper.

An old woman was making arrangements to bury her recently deceased husband. She spoke to the undertaker who asked her to give him a message. She thought about this for a while and said, "Jimmy is dead."

The undertaker reminded her that he needed six words.

The old woman pondered this for a few minutes before saying, "Jimmy is dead, car for sale."

An old age pensioners club were on a coach trip to Largs for the weekend. An old man was walking down the aisle of the coach when it lurches violently. The old man stumbles and lands in the lap of one of the female pensioners. In the resultant struggle, his elbow pokes the female pensioner in the breast.

Back on his feet he says: "I'm really sorry about that, but if your heart is as soft as your breast, I'm sure I'll see you in heaven."

The old woman replies: "And if your dick is as hard as your elbow, I'll see you in Largs."

Poor old Tam had just been put into a retirement home by his family and was feeling a bit sorry for himself. A young nurse came by his room and said, "Tam, it's no good moping about on a lovely sunny day like this. Why don't I take you onto the verandah where you can get a bit of fresh air?"

"Aye, ok then."

They go onto the verandah and Tam sits down.

After a few moments, Tam starts to lean over to his left so the nurse pushes him upright. After a couple of minutes, he leans over to his right and again the nurse straightens him up. Finally the nurse takes Tam back to his room.

The next day his family come to visit. They ask Tam is he is liking his new surroundings.

"Aye, well," says Tam, "The food's no bad, the bed is nice and soft and everybody is very friendly. The only problem is, they won't let you fart on the verandah."

"I finally stopped grandad from sliding down the banisters, mum." said the wee boy

"How did you manage to do that?" asked the boys mum.

"I wrapped barbed wire around it." the boy said

"WHAT!," said the boys mum, "Did that stop him?"

"Not exactly. But it does slow him down."

An army officer saw a busker playing a guitar at a London underground station. The busker had a sign which read:
VETERAN SOLDIER OF THE FALKLANDS WAR.
The officer thought, "Poor guy, I was there too and it was a living nightmare." He took £20 out of his wallet and gave it to the busker who said, "Gracias, senor."

Two old women are sitting outside their house having a quick smoke when it begins to rain. One of the old ladies takes out a condom, cuts the end of it and places it over the cigarette, keeping it nice and dry.

The other old lady asks what the strange thing is.

"It's a condom, Margaret"

"Where can you get them from, Rose?"

"Any good chemist sells them," said Margaret.

The next day, Margaret goes down to her local chemist and asks the pharmacist for a box of condoms. The pharmacist ask her what brand she would like to which the old woman replies, "I'm not really that bothered young man, as long as they'll fit a camel!"

A couple of old ladies were getting a bit bored in their retirement home one sunny afternoon. So they decided to liven things up a little by ripping their clothes off and streaking naked through the gardens. Two old men were sitting in the their deck chairs enjoying a bit of sun, when the old ladies flashed by.

"Did you see that, Billy?"

"Aye Wullie, but my eyes aren't what they used tae be. Whit were they wearin'?"

"Am no sure Billy, but whatever it was, they needed a bloody good iron."

A magician and his beautiful assistant are doing a live show in Glasgow. Part of the show featured a section where an audience member is invited onto the stage to perform their own trick.

A wee Glasgow man clambers onto the stage and says: "For ma trick, am gonna hiv te borrow yer lovely missus."

The guy whips off her skirt, pulls her pants down and starts to bang her from behind.

Outraged, the magician screams: "What the hell are you up to? That's no trick!"

The wee Glasgow man says: "Aye, ah know, but it's f****** magic!"

A guy emigrates to a remote part of Austalia to get away from the stresses and strains of the daily grind back home.

He finds a remote piece of farmland and settles in nicely.

One summers night though, the guy gets a knock on his door.

"G'Day mate, I'm Kanga Boomer. I'm yer nearest neighbour. I live on an old farmstead about 45 miles south of here."

"I'm having a party next Saturday night and I thought since you've been living out here all alone you might enjoy a party atmosphere, what d'ya say mate?"

The guy says, "Sure, that would be fantastic. I could do with a bit of company and some friendly chat. I've got a few crates of the ol' amber nectar I'll bring along."

Kanga says, "OK, but just ta warn ya, there will be drinking competitions, arm wrestling and a lot, and I mean a lot of wild sex going on. You're sure you still wanna come?"

"You make it sound like Heaven on earth Kanga." says the man.

"Whatever you say mate, there's only gonna be me and you there anyway. I'll see ya a eight o'clock."

What is the best way to catch Osama Bin Laden?
Load the warplanes with Viagara when they're bombing and hope the little prick stands up!

Not long after Mr Potato and Mrs Potato were married, they had a sweet little potato called Yam.

They both wanted the best for Yam and as she grew older, they warned her about going out and getting half baked because she could get mashed and people would call her a rotten potato.

Yam liked her food and would eat plenty so she wouldn't end up skinny like her cousins the French fries.

Young Yam grew up and wanted to see a bit of the world because she didn't want to stay at home and become a couch potato.

After travelling the world, Yam found the love of her life in the shape of Archie MacPherson. Mr. and Mrs. Potato horrified by this.

They wanted someone who would keep Yam in the style she had become accustomed to, someone with a lot of money.

They objected strongly to her to re-think her plans and told her she couldn't marry Archie because he was a common-tater!

A waiter brings the customer the steak he ordered with his thumb over the meat.

"Are you crazy?" yelled the customer, "with your hand on my steak?"

"What" answers the waiter, "You want it to fall on the floor again?"

Here are some questions to ponder:
● How come Superman could stop bullets with his chest, but always ducked when someone threw a gun at him?
● Why is it called a HAMBURGER, when it's made out of beef?
● Why does SOUR CREAM have an expiry date?
● What would a chair look like, if your knees bent the other way?
● Why is lemon juice made from artificial ingredients ... but washing up liquid contains real lemons.
● How much deeper would the ocean be, if sponges didn't grow in it.
● What do little birdies see, when they get knocked unconscious?

A guy was in his local curry house flicking through the menu. After several minutes he called the waiter over and said: "Excuse me, but could you explain this dish please?"

"Certainly sir," replied the waiter, what dish do you wish to know about?"

"This Lamb Tarka. Surely you mean Lamb Tikka?"

"Well sir, it is quite similar to Lamb Tikka but it's just a little otter."

There was once a Scotsman and an Englishman who lived next door to each other.

The Scotsman owned a hen and each morning he would eat one of the hens eggs for breakfast.

One day he couldn't find the hens egg and to his horror found that it had been laid in the Englishman's garden.

He was about to go next door when he saw the Englishman pick up the egg. The Scotsman ran up to the Englishman and told him that the egg belonged to himbecause he owned the hen. The Englishman disagreed because the egg was laid on his property.

They argued for a while until finally the Scotsman said: "In my family we solve any disputes like this: I kick you in the baws and time how long it takes you to get back up, then you kick me in the baws and time how long it takes for me to get up, whoever gets up quicker wins the egg."

The Englishman agreed to this, so the Scotsman found his pair of size 10, steel toe-capped Doc Martens, put them on and hoofed the Englishman full force right in the Rab Haws. The Englishman collapsed on the garden path clutching his swollen balls and howled in agony for 30 minutes.

Eventually the Englishman stood up and said, "Right, now it's my turn to kick you."

The Scotsman replied, "Nah, keep the egg."

A barber gave a haircut to a priest one day. The priest tried to pay for the haircut but the barber refused by saying: "I cannot accept money from you, you are a good man - you do God's work and help out with charitable organisations."

The next morning the barber found a dozen bibles at the door to his shop.

The next day, a police officer came to the barber for a haircut, and again the barber refused payment saying: "I cannot accept money from you, for you are a good man - you protect the public from harm."

The next morning the barber found a dozen doughnuts at the door to his shop.

Two days later, a lawyer came to the barber for a haircut, and again the barber refused payment saying: "I cannot accept money from you, for you are a good man - you serve the justice system."

The next morning the barber found a dozen more lawyers waiting for a haircut.

Two men held up a bank. They cleaned out all the cash drawers and then shoved all the clerks into the vault.

As they were getting ready to make their sharp exit, one of the clerks whispered: "Hey, would you do me a favour? Would you take the books, too? I'm five thousand short."

Two cannibals abduct a clown from the local circus, dice him up, throw him in the pot and then start to eat him.

Suddenly one of the cannibals looks at his friend and says. "Wait a minute. Does your meal taste a bit funny?"

Did you hear about the man who drowned in a bowl of museli? He was dragged under by a strong currant.

A small man is standing in a bar minding his own business when he notices a really tall man staring at him. The tall guy glances at the small guy and bellows, "Turner Brown, 8ft tall, 400 pounds with a 25 inch cock."

The small guy collapses on the floor, out for the count.

The big guy picks him up and shakes him gently bringing the small guy back into consciousness.

"What's wrong with you?" says the big guy.

"Look, what exactly did you say just there?"

"I said, Turner Brown, 8ft tall, 400 pounds with a 25 inch cock"

"Oh, thank God for that," said the small guy, "I thought you said 'turn around'."

Paddy and Mick are on a flight from Dublin to New York when the captain says:"Good afternoon everyone, I regret to inform you all that we have lost one of our engines. Don't worry, we have three more so there is nothing to worry about.

The only problem is that there will now be in the air for an extra 30 minutes. Thank you for your patience.

An hour later the captain announces that they have lost another engine and that an additional hour will be added to the journey.

Paddy and Mick aren't to happy with the situation because they will miss some serious drinking time in New York.

An hour later, the captain announces that they have now lost the third of the engines and that they will now be delayed two extra hours.

Paddy turns round to Mick and says. "Jesus Mick, at this rate we'll be up here all bloody night!"

In a courtroom a mugger was on trial. The victim was asked if she recognised the defendant. She said: "Yes that's him alright. I'd remember his face anywhere."

Unable to contain his anger, the accused jumped up and shouted: "She's lying! I was wearing a mask!"

A man was charged with lewd behaviour and public indecency, at court on Monday.

The suspect explained that as he was passing a pumpkin patch

he decided to stop. "You know, a pumpkin is soft and squishy inside, and there was no one around here for miles. At least I thought there wasn't," he stated in a phone interview.

The man went on to say that he pulled over to the side of the road, picked out a pumpkin that he felt was appropriate for his purposes, cut a hole in it, and proceeded to satisfy his need.

"I guess I was just really into it, you know?" he commented with evident embarrassment.

In the process, Lawrence apparently failed to notice a police car approaching and was unaware of his audience until officer approached him.

"It was an unusual situation" said the officer

"I walked up to him and he was still working away at this pumpkin."

"I said, 'Excuse me sir, but do you realise that you are screwing a pumpkin?"

"He froze and was clearly very surprised that I was there, and then looked me straight in the face and said."

"A pumpkin? Damn... is it midnight already?"

John Wayne Bobbitt has turned to the church for solace and has been ordained as a minister in Las Vegas. Rumour has it that his chapel has no organ.

A bloke decided to impress his new girlfriend with his knowledge of wine.

They went out to a posh restaurant and the guy asked for a bottle of vintage 1978 Italian Barollo. When the waiter returned with the wine, the man tasted it and said, "No this isn't right. This is a 1985 French Merlot! Bring me exactly what I ordered please."

The second bottle was poured and, once again the man was furious.

"Jesus H Christ! This is a 1985 alright, but it's a Cabernet Sauvignon from the South of France! Take it away!"

An old drunk was sitting at the bar of the restaurant watching the commotion. He staggered over to the couple's table and said: "You know, that's an amazing ability you have. Tell me, what's in this glass?"

The man took a sip. "Bloody hell, that tastes just like piss," he yelled as he spat a mouthful out.

"Hey, you're good," exclaimed the drunk. "Now can you tell me where I was born and how old I am?"

A guy walks into an expensive cake shop and asks for a donut. The guy behind the counter picks up a pair of tongs, uses it to pick up the donut and drops it into a small paper bag.

The customer is very impressed. "That's very hygienic using a pair of tongs."

"Yes sir, this is the cleanest cake shop in town."

"In that case I'll have a chocolate eclair as well."

Once again the assistant uses the tongs and picks up the eclair and drops it into another small paper bag.

While he is doing this, the customer notices a small piece of string sticking out of the shop assistants trousers. He asks, "Excuse me, but what is that string for?"

"Well sir, this is such a clean and hygienic shop that when I go to the toilet I'm not allowed to touch my penis so I pull it out with this piece of string."

The customer thinks about this for a moment and asks, "Tell me, how do you put it back in?"

"Oh that's easy," says the assistant, "I use the tongs."

A sandwich walks into a bar and orders a drink. The barman says, "Sorry, we don't serve food here."

When you go to court, just remember that you are trusting your fate to twelve people who weren't clever enough to get out of jury duty!

A couple are out having dinner in a restaurant.

A waitress who is standing at the next table notices the man is starting to slide off his chair. His partner continues to eat as if nothing strange was happening. The waitress continues to watch as the man slides right down off his chair and slides under the table.

"Excuse me" says the waitress,"I think your husband just slid under the table?"

The woman looked up at her and replied: "No he didn't. He's just walked in the door."

I ate in a chinese restaurant a few days ago. It was terrible. I called the waiter over and told him. "This bloody chicken is rubbery!"

He smiled at me and said, "Thank you berry much."

The most exciting part of a bulimic's birthday party is when the cake jumps out of the girl!

Knock, Knock
Who's there?
Canaloni.
Canaloni who?
It's canaloni here without you!

Two tubs of yogurt walk into a pub and order a couple of pints.

"No way," replies the barman, "There is no way I'm going to serve the likes of you!"

"Why not?," asks one of the yoghurts, "We're cultured individuals!"

A man is in a shop waiting to but a nice juicy cut of beef when the butcher asks him, "Excuse me, are you a gambling man?"

"I am," replies the customer.

"OK then, I bet you can't reach up and touch that meat hanging from the hooks." says the butcher.

"I'm not doing that" replies the customer, "I like a bet but the steaks are just to high."

A policeman stops a blonde woman who's been driving down the motorway.

"Excuse me miss, can I have a look at your drivers licence please?"

"A drivers licence, what on earth is that officer?"

"Well miss, it's a little piece of paper that has your details on it," says the policeman.

"Oh that!" she exclaims, "Yes, here it is."

"Can I have a look at your car insurance documentation too please miss?"

"I'm afraid I don't know what that is either officer."

"It's a document that says you're allowed to drive this car."

"Oh that. Duh! Here you officer. Sorry about that."

The policeman then unzips his trousers and the blonde says, "Oh my! Not another breathalyzer test."

Being overweight is something that just sort of snacks up on you.

A husband arrives home after a hard day at the office only to find his missus in bed with another man.

Outraged, he shouts: "Who the hell is this?"

"That's a good question," replied his wife, "What is your name anyway?"

A young businessman had rented out a beautiful office and had furnished it with antiques. Unfortunately, he had no business coming into his lovely office.

He was sitting at his antique desk when suddenly a man walked into the office.

Wanting to look busy, he picked up his phone and pretended he was negotiating a big deal, He spoke very loudly on the phone wanting to impress the guy who was now standing by his desk.

Finally he looked up at the stranger and said, "Sorry about that, can I help you with anything?"

The man replied, "Yes. I've come to install your telephone."

A woman and her friend were in town for lunch one afternoon when one of them said, "Look, there's my husband coming out of the florists with a huge bunch of flowers for me. Damn! That means I'll have to spend the rest of the week on my back with my legs in the air"

Her friend replied, "Would it not be easier if you got a vase for them instead?"

A woman was chatting to her neighbour over the garden fence on sunny morning. She said: "I feel fantastic today. In fact I felt so good this morning that I gave £10 to a bum."

"Really?" replied her friend, "What did your husband say about that?"

"He said thanks"

The TV is on the blink, so a woman calls a repairman. As he is about to finish the job, the woman hears her husbands key in the door.

She says to the repairman, "Look, I'm really sorry but my husband is a really jealous guy. If he finds you here, he'll fly into a rage and beat you into a pulp. You've got to find somewhere to hide."

The repairman looks about him and decides to hide in the back of the TV set.

When the husband goes into the living room, he slumps down in front of the TV and switches it on to watch the football.

Inside the TV, the repairman is getting hotter and hotter and is close to suffocating so he thinks, "Bugger this, I'm out of here."

So he clambers out of the TV, strides across the living room and out of the front door.

The wife looks on in horror at her husband who says: "Jeez, I must be whacked, I don't remember the referee sending that guy off!"

A truck driver stops on the motorway to give a young woman a lift.
"Hop on in. I'm not like all the other truckers who only give rides to the good looking girls."

In the Garden of Eden, God called Adam over.

"Now Adam, I am going to teach you how to kiss a beautiful woman."

After God had told Adam what to do, he went over and kissed Eve.

God called him back over and said, "Now Adam, I am going to teach you how to make love with a beautiful woman."

After God had told Adam what to do, Adam approached Eve.

A minute later, Adam came back to God and said, "Lord, what is a headache?"

A guy went into a bookshop and asked the salesgirl if she had a book called, "How to Master Your Wife."

The salesgirl said: "Our science fiction section is upstairs."

A woman awoke with a start one night and discovered her husband was cramming a bottle of asprins into her mouth.

She spat them out and screamed, "What the hell do you think you're doing? Are you trying to kill me?"

"Do you have a headache?" asked the husband.

"No I bloody well don't." the wife fumed.

"Great," said the husband, "Let's have a shag!"

A guy goes to his doctor and is told that he only has one more day to live.

The guy is distraught, but his wife decides she had better be nice to him and tells him they can make love all night long.

After the fourth time that night, the woman is starting to get a wee bit bored and says: "Listen, I know you want to keep shagging, but unlike you, I have to get up in the morning!"

How do you know when you're REALLY ugly?
Dogs hump your leg with their eyes closed.

It was the day of the big sale. Rumors of the sale were the main reason for the long line that formed by 8:30, the store's opening time, in front of the store.

A small man pushed his way to the front of the line, only to be pushed back, amid loud and colourful curses. On the man's second attempt, he was punched square in the jaw, and knocked around a bit, and then thrown to the end of the line again.

As he got up the second time, he said to the person at the end of the line...

"That does it! If they hit me one more time, I don't open the store!"

Upon entering the little country store, the stranger noticed a sign saying; DANGER! BEWARE OF DOG! posted on the glass door. Inside he noticed a harmless old hound dog asleep on the floor besides the cash register.

He asked the store manager: "Is THAT the dog folks are supposed to beware of?"

"Yup, that's him," he replied.

The stranger couldn't help but be amused. "That certainly doesn't look like a dangerous dog to me. Why in the world would you post that sign?"

"Because"; the owner replied, "before I posted that sign, people kept tripping over him."

Why did the cat cross the road?
It was the chicken's day off.

A man went to the zoo and was standing in front of the lion cage looking at the lions. He suddenly noticed one lion was in the back corner of the cage furiously licking the bottom of another lion.

He quickly called for the zoo keeper and ask if the lion was sick.

The zoo keeper said: "No, a group of Rangers fans came through a little while ago and one of the fans fell in and the lion ate him.

The visitor was still confused and the zoo keeper said: "Don't worry, he's just trying to get the taste out of his mouth!

An explorer in the deepest Amazon suddenly finds himself surrounded by a bloodthirsty group of cannibals. Upon surveying the situation, he says quietly to himself: "Oh God, I'm screwed."

The sky darkens and a voice booms out: "No, you are NOT screwed. Pick up that stone at your feet and bash in the head of the chief standing in front of you."

So with the stone he bashes the life out of the chief. Standing above the lifeless body, breathing heavily looking at 100 angry natives...

The voice booms out again, "Okay... NOW you're screwed."

I had a terrible fight with my wife. I said, "You know, you're going to drive me to my grave." In two minutes she had the car in front of the house.

A little turtle begins to climb a tree slowly. After long hours of effort, he reaches the top, jumps into the air waving his front legs, until reaches heavily into the ground with a hard knock over his shell. After recovering his consciousness, he starts to climb the tree again, jumps again, and knocks the ground heavily again. The little turtle insisted again and again after each knock, while a couple of birds sitting at the edge of a branch, looking the turtle with pain. suddenly the female bird says to the male: "Hey dear, I think it's time to tell our little turtle he is adopted"

My cousin Jane is the world's worst at getting instructions mixed up. When she got married her husband bought her one of those fancy, electric coffee makers. It had all the latest gadgets on it. The salesman carefully explained how everything worked; how to plug it in, set the timer, go back to bed, and upon rising, the coffee is ready."

A few weeks later Jane was back in the store and the salesman asked her how she liked her coffee maker.

"Wonderful!" she replied, "However, there's one thing I don't understand. Why do I have to go to bed every time I want to make a pot of coffee?"

What do you do if a blonde throws a grenade at you?
  Take the pin out and throw it back.

It was their first date, and she'd shown the patience of a saint as he babbled on and on about his hobbies. Finally, he came up for air and said: "But enough about me. Let's talk about you."

She breathed a sigh of relief.

He went on, "What do you think about me?"

Two men were sitting next to each other at a bar.

After a while, one guy looks at the other and says: "I can't help but think, from listening to you, that you're from Ireland."

The other guy responds proudly: "Yes, that I am!"

The first guy says: "So am I! And where about from Ireland might you be?"

The other guy answers: "I'm from Dublin, I am."

The first guy responds: "Sure and begora, and so am I! And what street did you live on in Dublin?"

The other guy says: "A lovely little area it was, I lived on McCleary Street in the old central part of town."

The first guy says: "Faith and it's a small world. So did I! And to what school would you have been going?"

The other guy answers: "Well now, I went to St. Mary's of course."

The first guy gets really excited, and says: "And so did I. Tell me, what year did you graduate?"

The other guy answers: "Well, now, I graduated in 1964."

The first guy exclaims: "The Good Lord must be smiling down upon us! I can hardly believe our good luck at winding up in the same bar tonight. Can you believe it, I graduated from St. Mary's in 1964 my own self."

About this time, another guy walks into the bar, sits down, and orders a beer.

The bartender walks over shaking his head and mutters: "It's going to be a long night tonight, the Murphy twins are drunk again."

An English professor was lecturing to his class one day.

"In English," he said, "a double negative forms a positive. In some languages, though, such as Russian, a double negative is still a negative. However, there is no language wherein a double positive can form a negative."

A voice from the back of the room piped up, "Yeah, right."

Teacher: Why are you late?
Pupil: Because of the sign.
Teacher: What sign?
Pupil: The one that says, "School Ahead, Go Slow."

The crusty old managing partner finally passed away, but his firm kept receiving calls asking to speak with him. "I'm sorry, he's dead," was the standard answer.

Finally, the receptionist who fielded the calls began to realise it was always the same voice, so she asked who it was and why he kept calling. The reply: "I used to work for peanuts and he made my life hell, and I just like to hear you say it."

The CIA loses track of one of its operatives, and so calls in one of their top spy hunters

The CIA boss says: "All I can tell you is that his name is Murphy and that he's somewhere in Ireland. If you think you've located him, tell him the code words, 'The weather forecast calls for mist in the morning.'

"If it's really him, he'll answer, 'Yes, and for mist at noon as well.'"

So the spy hunter goes to Ireland and stops in a bar in one of the small towns. He says to the barman: "Maybe you can help me. I'm looking for a guy named Murphy."

The bartender replies: "You're going to have to be more specific because, around here, there are lots of guys named Murphy.

"There's Murphy the Baker, who runs the pastry shop on the next block. There's Murphy the Banker, who's president of our local savings bank. There's Murphy the Blacksmith, who works at the stables.

"And, as a matter of fact, my name is Murphy, too."

Hearing this, the spy hunter figures he might as well try the code words on bartender, so he says, "The weather forecast calls for mist in the morning."

The bartender replies: "Oh, you're looking for Murphy the Spy. He lives right down the street."

Reverend Billy Graham tells of a time early in his ministry when he arrived in a small town to preach a sermon.

Wanting to mail a letter, he asked a young boy where the post office was. When the boy had told him, Dr. Graham thanked him and said: "If you'll come to the Baptist Church this evening, you can hear me telling everyone how to get to Heaven."

"I don't think I'll be there," the boy said. "You don't even know your way to the post office."

The regular foursome teed off on time that Saturday morning. On the second hole Joe noticed a funeral procession going by and stopped, held his hat over his heart and bowed his head.
His partners noticed and complimented Joe on his thoughtfulness.
"Well, She was a good wife for 40 years," replied Joe.

A man went camping in the woods by himself.

He awoke early in the morning to hear a strange growling sound. He looked out to see a bear. He immediately began to run as fast as he could.

The bear was gaining on him and he finally gave up hope, fell on his knees and said: "Oh God, please let this be a Christian bear!"

He turned to see the bear on his knees saying: "Lord bless this food I am about to receive!"

A blind man was travelling in his private jet when he detected something was wrong. He made his way to the cockpit and got no response from his pilot.

The blind guy then found the radio and started calling the tower. "Help! Help!"

The tower came back and asked what was wrong.

The blind guy says: "Help Me! I'm blind, the pilot is dead, and we're flying upside down!"

The tower comes back and asks: "How do you know you're upside down?"

The blind guy replies: "Because the SHIT is running up my back!"

A market researcher called at a house and his knock was answered by a young woman with three small children running around her. He asked her if she minded replying to his questions.

When she said no, he mentioned that among their many products was Vaseline and she certainly knew of that product. When asked if she used it, the answer was "yes." Asked how she used it she said: "To assist my husband and I in conjugal matters."

The interviewer was amazed. He said: "I always ask that question because everyone uses our product and they always say they use it for the child's bicycle chain, or the gate hinge; but I know that most use it for conjugal matters. Since you've been so frank, could you tell me exactly how you use it?"

"Yes, we put it on the door handle to keep the kids out."

One afternoon, a man was riding in the back of his limousine when he saw two men eating grass by the road side. He ordered his driver to stop and he got out to investigate. "Why are you eating grass," he asked one man.

"We don't have any money for food," the poor man replied.

"Oh, come along with me then."

"But sir, I have a wife with two children!"

"Bring them along! And you, come with us too," he said to the other man.

"But sir, I have a wife with six children," the second man answered.

"Bring them as well!"

They all climbed into the car, which was no easy task, even for a car as large as the limo.

Once underway, one of the poor fellows says: "Sir, you are too kind. Thank you for taking all of us with you."

The rich man replied: "No, you don't understand, the grass at my home is about two meters tall!"

Did you hear about the Veterinarian and the Taxidermist who combined their business?
Their slogan: "Either way you get your pet back."

Why does a tiger have stripes?
So he won't be spotted.

What do you call a cat who does tricks?
A magic kit.

**Why should you walk carefully when it's raining cats and dogs?
You might step in a poodle.**

What kind of work does a weak cat do?
Light mouse work.

Why did the mother cat put stamps on her kittens?
Because she wanted to mail a litter.

Which game did the cat want to play with the mouse?
Catch.

Where did the kittens go on their class trip?
To a mewseum.

Why did the blone climb up to the roof of the bar? She heard that the drinks were on the house.

A blonde walked into a shoe shop wanting to buy some new alligator shoes. The salesman quoted a price of £250.

The guy replied: "This is an outrage. There is no way I will pay that kind of money for a pair of shoes. I can shoot an alligator and get shoes for less than that."

The salesman answered: "Well, lady, I think you should do that."

Later that day, the salesman was driving and found the blonde standing waist deep in the swamp with a rifle pointed at a huge, mean-looking alligator swimming toward her. She pointed the gun and shot it, then dragged it out of the water.

The salesman was surprised to see 20 dead alligators lying on their backs.

The blonde rolled the alligator over she had just shot and exclaimed: "SHIT! That one isn't wearing shoes either!"

What's the difference between an intelligent blonde and a UFO?
Don't know, I haven't seen either.

This is a story of four people named Everybody, Somebody, Anybody and Nobody.

There was an important job to be done and Everybody was sure that Somebody would do it.

Anybody could have done it, but Nobody did it.

Somebody got angry about that because it was Everybody's job. Everybody thought Anybody could do it, but Nobody realised that Everybody wouldn't do it.

It ended up that Everybody blamed Somebody when Nobody did what Anybody could have done!

There were two boys that were always into trouble and any time something went wrong people assumed they did it.

Their parents went to a minister who was successful in sorting out kids he said: "Okay, I'll help. Send in the youngest kid tomorrow and the older one the next day."

The young kid went in and the man asked him: "Where is God?"

The boy didn't answer so the man said a little louder: "WHERE IS GOD?"

The kid didn't answer so the man yelled: "WHERE IS GOD?"

The kid got really scared so he ran all the way home and locked himself in the toilet. His brother heard the door slam so he said: "Hey whats wrong."

So the younger one let him in and said: "We're in big trouble now, God is missing and they think we have him."

Why did the fish get turned down by the Army?
He failed his herring test.

A mine owner is looking for new guys to do some
necessary jobs, so he advertised and three guys
turned up.

One is a big muscular Irish guy, the other is an
Italian guy and the last one is Japanese.

The owner tells the Irish guy that he will be in
charge of the mining because he is strong,. The
Italian will be in charge of the money and the
Japanese, because he is good with numbers will be
in charge of the supplies.

In the next morning everybody is coming to work
and someone is counting the people going into the
mine… 200 people.

Everything goes well and at the end of the day
they do not want to leave anybody in the mine so
they count the people who go out… 199.

They went back to look for the last one. They were
looking for a few hours and then just before they
were about to leave the Japanese guy jumped from
behind the rock shouting: "SUPPLIES! SUPPLIES!"

What do you get when you cross a parrot with a
centipede?
A walkie-talkie.

A couple attending an art exhibition at the National Gallery were staring at a portrait that had them completely confused.

The painting depicted three very black and totally naked men sitting on a park bench.

Two of the figures had black penises, but the one in the middle had a pink penis.

The curator of the gallery realized that they were having trouble interpreting the painting and offered his assessment.

He went on for nearly half an hour explaining how it depicted the sexual emasculation of African-Americans in a predominately white, patriarchal society.

"In fact," he pointed out, "some serious critics believe that the pink penis also reflects the cultural and sociological oppression experienced by gay men in contemporary society."

After the curator left, a Welshman approached the couple and said: "Would you like to know what the painting is really about?"

"Now why would you claim to be more of an expert than the curator of the gallery," asked the couple.

"Because I'm the guy who painted it," he replied. "In fact, there's no African-Americans depicted at all. They're just three Welsh coal-miners.

"The only difference is that the guy in the middle went home for lunch."

Books available from our collection:

The 2003 Crossword Book	£5.99
The 2003 Tam Cowan Joke Book	£5.99
Lorenzo Amoruso: LA Confidential (paperback)	£9.99
Lorenzo Amoruso: LA Confidential (hardback)	£17.99

All these books are available at your local bookshop or newsagent, or can be ordered direct. Indicate the number of copies required and fill in the form below.

Send to: *First Press Publishing,*
Daily Record and Sunday Mail,
1 Central Quay,
Glasgow, G3 8DA

or phone: **08000 567 400** quoting title, author and credit or debit card number.

or fax: **0141 309 1430**, quoting title, author and credit or debit card number.

or email: **orders@first-press.co.uk**

Enclose a remittance* to the value of the cover price plus 75p per book for postage and packing. European customers allow £1.50 per book for post and packing.

* Payment may be made in sterling by UK personal cheque, Eurocheque, postal order, sterling draft or international money order, made payable to First Press Publishing.

Alternatively by Visa/Mastercard/Debit Card Card No.

Expiry Date ☐☐☐☐   Valid From Date ☐☐☐☐   Issue Number ☐

Signature: _____

Applicable only in the UK and BFPO addresses.

While every effort is made to keep prices low, it is sometimes necessary to increase prices at short notice. First Press Publishing reserve the right to show on covers and charges new retail prices which may differ from those advertised in the text or elsewhere.

NAME AND ADDRESS (IN BLOCK CAPITALS PLEASE)

Name _____

Address _____

_____

_____Postcode_____

TMG will use your information for administration and analysis. We may share it with carefully selected third parties. We, or they, may send you details of goods and services. The information may be provided by letter, telephone or other. If you do not want your details to be shared please tick this box.

Volume 2

Rhapsody : SASMAC I